Copyright © 2014 Aletta Hodges

Published by Cinematic Ink Publications

Dangerously In Love

"Blame it on the Streets"

By

Aletta H.

<u>DEDICATION</u>

I had my first child at 15 and three more to follow by the time I was 22. I am a 38 year old grandmother of four and I am thankful. I'm thankful for that experience, that challenge God set forth because now I can help others, including my own child as a young single mother. I learned how to love someone more than I loved myself. I learned patience. I grew. I found me through them. I learned how to pray. I used to say I gave them my whole life and now I realize they gave me life and I'm thankful. I want to dedicate this book to my smart, beautiful, highly favored children Mylisha, Ahjah, Benasia, and Robert. I love you for life!

INTRODUCTION

Hi, I'm Reminisce, a young mother. Struggling to raise my children and put the pieces of my life back together. Please take this journey with me as I tell my story....

CHAPTER 1
THE BEGINNING OF THE END

Woke

Wake up; wake up it was only a dream
All that has happen, such horrible things.
Open your eyes wide now and see all that u can see
Horrible things can no longer come to be.
Listen; listen to dat lil whisper in your head
Ignored repeating messages said.
Get up; get up suddenly knocked off your feet
Get a grip, take a breath, relax, have a seat.
Subliminal messages everywhere you turn
Blindsided later lessons to be learned.
Shhhh, don't yell no words spoken now,
Emotional words come from deep down.
Be still don't move no reaction at all
Just a complaint over something already saw.
All that has happen, oh such horrible things
Wake up, wake up it was only a dream.

Jimmy and I were back together. I really thought I was never getting back with him, he was a butthole. Jimmy cheated on me all the time. He was a control freak. We had been on and off for about 4 years and by this time I had grown accustom to the lifestyle being with him afforded me. The drug money supported my children and I would do anything for my children, even if it meant putting up with all the abuse as long as they were okay. This break up was a little different. I was upset because he let his friends talk to me anyway, just plain ole disrespectful. The worst part is that whenever I would bring it to Jimmy's attention, he chose the side of his partners in crime, so I left. He was in business with them so he chose money over me.

After a week of begging and me being low on cash I surrendered. I got scared. I didn't believe in myself enough to make it on my own. I spent the whole day with the Africans getting my brains pulled out with blonde zillions, it was Jimmy's preferred hairstyle on me. I emptied the house of the kids and cleaned it. I took forever getting ready. I got dressed to perfection. I wore a pink sequin shirt that was form fitting and sum black leggings with pink sequin red bottoms. I knew deep down that this was the wrong thing to do. I was at a low point in my life though and I needed the attention.

Jimmy arrived about 11:30 that night with a bottle of Patron and sum pineapple juice and grabbed the remote. Jimmy kept his phone in his hand, texting and taking calls, talking in code. I was holding my tongue just wanting to relax and enjoy the evening. We talked for a while and he told me all the things I wanted to hear. I surrendered myself, my being, my soul to him.

As the night grew and the alcohol was sitting in, we start to get a little more comfortable. I could see pain in his eyes. A lot of the time it felt like I was protecting him from himself so it gave me a soft spot for him. I knew his story and he knew mine and we accepted each other's flaws. We reminisced about good times and laughed. Jimmy laid his hand on the small of my back and I melted in his arms.

THUMP...... THUMP THUMP THUMP.......BANG.

Just as things were about to get heated up when four masked men came rushing through the back door all brandishing big metal objects in their hands. Jimmy got up and rushed toward the masked men and I froze. I watch strikes to Jimmy's head and blood pouring down his face as he fought for his life and I couldn't move. One of the large masked men approaches me and started to swing repeatedly at my head and body causing me to fall to the floor. With blood blinding me, I balled up into a fetal position and prepare to die. I heard footsteps and the door open. I remain still praying the blows to my body stop. Everything became completely silent.

One of my eyes was completely swollen shut; I wiped the other in an attempt to see what was going on. I notice that the front door was open and I could hear Jimmy yelling outside. I tried to stand but it was of no use. My hand was swollen and felt as if I was wearing a baseball mitt from trying to cover my face. My legs were unrecognizable and I couldn't feel any pain. I was scared to go outside so I drug myself over to the couch and started digging for my phone in the couch.

Apparently the masked men ran out when they saw someone pull up at neighbors' and Jimmy ran outside for help. The adrenaline was pumping through my system like a freight train, I managed to somehow run up the stairs not knowing my leg was broken to check on my youngest daughter who was 14. I was relieved to see she was still asleep in bed and hadn't heard a thing. All my children either sleep walked, talked, or something to do with sleep, so it wasn't out of the ordinary for her to be still asleep. I screamed her name and she jumped up screaming after seeing blood pouring down my face. Jimmy ran up the stairs behind me also blood pouring from his head we all were panicking. We all proceeded back down the stairs. I felt my leg give out half way down the stairs. I lifted it off the steps and hopped down and sat on the couch. I was trembling so hard my teeth were chattering.

I found my phone and called the police. Once the ambulance arrived and finally got us to the hospital I was relieved. After we were rushed into the emergency room, the police wanted to question me and Jimmy about what had happened but I had no answers to give them. The cast was put on my leg and they finished stitching my head which now had about 15 zillions left. By the grace of God I didn't feel any pain, it was like I was carried the whole time. Jimmy had 17 staples in his head and two missing teeth. I called my sister to come get us from the hospital and after she picked us up we got dropped off to a hotel. All I could think was how I am going to see my father at the hospice home tomorrow like this it will kill him.

****

I was paranoid sleeping at the hotel, I felt like someone was watching me. Reality hadn't set in on all that had occurred the prior night. I sobbed repeatedly while Jimmy tried to comfort me I wasn't thinking about my wounds. I was thinking how am I going to face my father in his death bed his favorite person my favorite person far from okay. I couldn't believe God was putting me through all this, I was a good girl. I was daddy's girl. I got straight A's in school, I loved band but life happened. I had sex one time and I got pregnant and my life changed forever.

Normal as a child for me consisted of garbage bags full of packaged marijuana. Different size baggies rolled to perfection using the whole bag lining the weed at the bottom. There were boosters with different clothes and household supplies stopping by daily. Normal for me as a child was pulling up in a blinged out white Cadillac with red interior to school with McDonald's for breakfast and four crisp dollars for lunch. The kids at school would ask me was my daddy a pimp. I didn't dress girly but kept a fresh pair of pink K Swiss or all white dope mans with the pink swoosh. The boosters kept us clean. I laughed from all the questions about my father. I never told our family business though I kept them guessing. We had money most of the time but no one worked. That garbage bag full of weed took care of everything. There were women in his face all the time but he loved my mother, he was just street. He hustled and he hustled hard to take care of us, especially me.

I was a good girl but life happened. I was his twin and our personalities were similar. In my eyes, my father could do no wrong even if he was wrong.

I would side with him which put a wedge between me and other family members. We had barbeques all summer and most winters. I was the youngest of four children and there was a ten year difference between me and my oldest sibling. I had two sisters and a brother. My brother who had been in and out of jail had found a white girl off the street and fell in love with her. He had dabbled in drugs but eventually got his life together and had a degree, a wife and family. My brother was one of the few that overcame an addiction.

There was only me and my sister still home by the time I was 12. I remember one night we were upstairs washing our hair, laughing. We always laughed, we were happy kids. Our parents were both comically talented so we were the same. On this particular night, we were dancing around the bathroom singing *Pretty Young Thang* by Michael Jackson, laughing at how bad we sounded. All of a sudden we heard a loud voices, dogs and chaos downstairs. Me and my sister paused.

"This better not be Big Gems playing because that's not funny. He always come over here joking around." I said.

"ANYBODY UPSTAIR PLEASE COME DOWN WITH YOUR HANDS UP" A voice shouted.

I was shocked to hear that declaration; I was 12 and had soap in my hair. I didn't know what was going on. Two officers rush through the door; guns pointed and manhandle us down the stairs.

"Wait! Wait! There are dogs in here. I'm scared to death of dogs. Daddy help!" I cried out.

For as long as I could remember I had been afraid of dogs, I didn't know why. I was terrified. In my eyes dogs were a gorilla, a bear they intimidated me. My mother and father were on the floor with their hands cuffed behind their back. My mother was crying but my father held an icy blank stare. Once he realized I was crying, shaking because of the police dogs everywhere, he pleaded with the police to take us outside. They placed us on the couch while German shepherds roamed through our home.

I closed my eyes and shook so hard until I felt urine flow down the Hammer pants I was just dancing in, laughing moments ago. My sister wrapped her arms around me to shield my face. Once my dad saw that he began to scream.

"Take them outside, they're kids" He demanded.

They refused even though they saw my tear filled eyes. He explained to them my fear of dogs and how frightened I was and eventually a female officer agreed. She saw I wasn't handling it well and called two officers. They escorted us outside where two more officers were located. I blacked everything out but the dogs after that.

My father spent a few years in prison and got out and continued hustling but was forced to maintain employment so he worked at a factory the later part of me growing up. He still maintained our family but him and my mother fought a lot. They were so accustomed to the drug money it was hard to live a check to check life.

My grandfather would come over with his sawed off shot gun threatening my father's life if he hit my mother again. It didn't matter my mother wasn't leaving him. I saw him pull his belt off and whoop her like a child. In my mind I thought she must have done something to deserve it. I took his side not knowing later in life I would face the same humiliating emotional and physical abuse she did. I thought since she didn't leave it wasn't a big deal. They were both attractive people and got a lot of attention from the opposite sex so it hindered their relationship.

My father was a classy guy. He stayed fresh in some creased slacks and a crisp shirt with white gold jewelry on including both ears. He wore a Dobb, Kangol or some other brand hat at all times and he kept on his dark shades. He was my hero. He was next to God to me and I didn't think I could be any luckier. I talked to my father about everything. I learned early that I couldn't lie to him. He could look at me and tell. My father would take me everywhere with him so he could hear people say how much we looked alike. We weren't close to his mother, her and my mother didn't get along so we only saw her on holidays. My father loved his mother and spent a lot of time with her. When she passed my mother was asked to go to the funeral home and do her hair and makeup. I went with my mother. I wasn't scared since it was my father's mother lying there on a white mat covered with a white sheet with her neck and head exposed. There was a light dangling on top that lit that area of the dark funeral home. My mother paused as she walked in the door and said she left her small curling irons outside. I grabbed the other bag and walked over to the table and started to set up my makeup.

My grandmother and I looked the same she was just older. I wondered was that how I was going to look when I died. She was a beautiful caramel complexion with a white women's pointy nose. She had full round lips and broad eyes. I didn't even notice that my mother didn't return until I was finished framing her face in spiral curls with a pearl hair pin. My father was proud of me for doing that and she looked beautiful. It made him cry seeing her. Our relationship was close after that because he knew I had his back too.

My mother was high yellow with deep dimples a small waist and huge butt. She resembled Jackie Brown always wearing bra top and short shorts. My father was street but he couldn't top my mother, she was straight gangster. She had been shot in her face and would shoot someone in theirs. Her beefs were serious, family and all. She had a spat with her sister and waited two days with a nine on her porch for her sister to drive down the alley. When my aunt did drive down, my mother let the whole clip loose and they sped away luckily uninjured. She didn't carry herself that way she was a diva her hair stayed died in blond streaks, her nails stayed manicured and painted, she wore delicate gold chains and bracelets. She was stunning. It broke my mother's heart to have to tell my father I was pregnant at 15. My mother was ready to drop the cash on an abortion. My father swore never to speak to me again if I did, he said it was murder. I believed him and kept her.

CHAPTER 2

Not thinking before I think,

DE attaching links.
Not thinking of other first,

Ending up hurt.
Right before my eyes,

A childhood dies.
Butterflies inside

Knowing why.
Not paying attention to life.
Letting it pass me by.
Not even fighting the fight of good,

Never understood.
Fighting demons

Control my being,

Not seeing.
Knowing wrong

Just not being strong.
Acting

Not realizing the cost.
Once again I've lost.
Wishing I could turn back time

Rewind.
All the mistakes I've made

Wishing I could trade.
Older emotions run deep,

No release.
So many chances only to lose another,

Hurting others.
Throwing life up in a toss,

Once again I've lost.

Aletta H.

My grandmother always told me it was almost a curse to be nice and she was cursed with that too. She said I will endure a lot of pain through life because I'm blessed with patience and a big loyal heart. My grandmother, my mother's mother, was a god to all of us. I swear this lady had powers. I would have nose bleeds and she would take me to her bedroom and pray for me and it would stop. My grandmother was praying constantly. She had an aura about her that made you know everything was going to be alright when you entered her home no matter what it was. I didn't find out until her funeral that she was a Mason. I heard humming coming from the back of the church during her service and turned around to see the whole back of the church was filled with women in all white. They were covering the whole back wall standing in attention with their hands folded in front of them. They had on nurse type hats with pins all over there military type uniforms that consisted of a white jacket, white skirt, stockings and white gloves.

My grandmother laid in her casket like a queen with the same attire on filled with pins and ribbons like she was high in ranks of the masonry. I was used to seeing her in a smock type gown with snaps all the way up and house shoes but never in that. I had no clue what it all meant but I knew she was important. As the service was coming to an end the humming got louder and the women started walking up the aisles it was amazing. Four men in all black suits with pins all over them also carried the queen's casket out. I wanted to know more about it but everything was so secret. I just knew she belonged to them.

I spent a lot of time in my grandmother's kitchen helping her cook, shucking corn off the cob or scaling fish she'd just caught; I learned to cook early. There was newspaper some days all over the floor while we picked stems off of greens. There were a lot of BBQs at her house and all the kids would play around the house. My grandfather wasn't used to city life. He had ducks and a dog chained in the back. I've never been into animals, so I stayed in with my grandmother. I had tons of cousins and because my grandmother had nine children we were all close like siblings.

I wasn't a pretty girl. When I went through puberty I was fat and dark. I did the all-time no no and switched from a perm to a curl and lost the little hair I had so I sported extensions after that. I resembled a smaller version of Fat Albert with braids. I would go swimming and tan dark and by the winter I was caramel with dark spots left. It was hard to adjust to my own appearance. I had a cute face but the rest of me was whack. My sisters both had my mother's figure so I was jealous. They both looked like models and I looked more like their little brother. I didn't complain about it though, I made up for it in intellect. I was smart as a whip and I played 8 instruments successfully while I was in junior high, mastering the flute and piccolo.

I loved to type. I took practical office training to opt out of gym and realized I was comfortable in there. When I was twelve my father bought me a pink and white word processor so I would write anonymous poems to my teachers and they would post them on their walls. No one knew it was me but me. I didn't want the attention, it just felt good to know my teachers enjoyed them.

Aletta H.

I wrote a poem for my civics teacher called teach peace. He made copies for several other teachers and they posted them too.

Teach peace teach peach. Let us not decrease into a world of madness, children feeling nothing but sadness, forgetting the innocence in laughter, teach from your heart, give children a proper start, there's nowhere else for them to seek if you teach peace. Dig deep get beneath, what they see with their eyes, societal lies. Popularity doesn't determine their lives. What they wear just covering there cries. Material compensated for their fatherless lives. All the teachers sit down to a feast make the subject of the feast teach peace teach peace.

Poems fell out of me. I would write short stories and songs constantly. Words and phrases would engulf my mind. Anything I was going through I could take it out my mind and place it on paper and close it out. I was kind of a nerd but I didn't get teased though. I had a great personality and was funny, so I had a lot of friends. I worked a summer job that was provided for low income students with a lot of my friends. It was nice to have a check and buy my own things. To lessen the burden of my family was a big deal to me. My family knew I was going to be successful. I developed a work ethic that wasn't taught to me. It was who I was.

One of my friends asked me to babysit with her one evening and I agreed. She said her brother and his friend were here from a nearby city and they were coming over. I was excited I hadn't even kissed a boy and I was almost 15. After work I walked to her cousins where she was babysitting and I tried to look more like a girl.

I put on a tennis skirt and a pink hoodie to match with some pink and white dope man Nikes. I pulled my poetic justice braid through a hole that I pulled through a pink and white Nike cap. I was clean and it looked like I came from money and I was comfortable in the skin I was in. When I got there I was surprised the guys had already arrived and she had already been babysitting. There were 3 forty ounces of Old E on the table and some Seagram's gin. I was shy and couldn't calm down so I let my friend talk me into having a drink, which led to finishing all the drinks with everybody else and was wasted for the first time.

I feel confident, sexy. I was feeling some type of way about her brother and the feeling was mutual. We sat close on the couch and giggled as he touched my itty bitty breast trapped in this big body and I felt like I was wetting my panties. He started kissing me and I couldn't control the urge coming in my panties. He put his fingers between my legs and it was over.

I allowed him on top of me and he slid my big girl panties to the side and put it in.

"OUCH... OUCH! This ain't that fun." I whined thinking he could just hurry up.

I felt like I was going to throw up. It wasn't at all what I expected, but he was having fun. I didn't even move I was tense. I could feel a stinging sensation down there like he tore me open. His sweat was dripping on my face as he forced himself inside my untouched vagina. When he slumped off of me, I ran to the bathroom and splashed water on my face.

I grabbed a towel to clean myself and it hurt. I tried to pee and it stung so bad, I jumped up and pee flowed down my leg. I was grossed out and I was scared.

"What did I just do?" I said to myself, drunk and staggering all over the bathroom trying to clean pee off my leg.

I staggered back to the living room and fell on the couch. Luckily, they'd left and we disposed the liquor bottles and went to sleep. I was in and out of sleep because of the pain. I threw up a few times and sobbed to myself. My head was banging. I tried to forget it. I lost my virginity to a stranger. In my mind it didn't happen, it was a dream, a bad dream. A few weeks had past and I was in my daily routine, work, library and home. I felt horrible for that night and I never wanted to see him again.

While at work one day with the same friend I started to feel sick. I threw up outside, I thought I had a summer flu. She joked about me being pregnant but after a week of throwing up I thought about it too. No way would God let that happen to me. You don't get pregnant the first time. She talked me into going to get tested and it came out positive. I couldn't believe it, I couldn't cry. I couldn't tell my parents. I was scared and wanted a do over. I knew I couldn't alter God's plans and have an abortion. I just had to continue.

I called my oldest sister to try and convince her to call and tell my mother the health department called and said I was pregnant but she refused. She said I had to tell her myself.

I just knew my mother was going to beat the brakes off me. I got home and told my middle sister and she agreed to tell my mother as long as I was there when she told her. I agreed.

"Mom Reminisce has something to tell you." My sister declared instead of doing as she agreed.

My heart hit the floor, I was bracing myself for her hit. Tears filled my eyes as I began to speak.

"Mom I'm pregnant." I whispered.

"Yeah right, you haven't even had a boyfriend." She replied.

My mother realized I was serious when I showed her the paperwork and the information the health department had given me and collapsed to the ground. She started screaming at me.

"You're not having it! I'm not taking care of anymore kids." She screamed at me.

My mother had her first child at 15 also and she was tired. She knew how that would affect my life. She knew my straight A's meant nothing if I was to have a child now. She called my father and he pulled up. I could see the disappointment all over his face.

I felt ashamed and dirty. I thought he was going to look at me different but he didn't. My father said if I had an abortion he would disown me. He said that was a quick fix I would have to live with forever and he would do any and everything to raise her.

Nine months later, I gave birth to a healthy beautiful little chubby girl who looked just like me but better. By me being so young. I passed out during birth and they had to rush me to critical care. I woke up 3 days later hooked up to everything. My mother stood over me crying. I didn't realize days had passed. I reached down and saw my stomach was gone and asked to see my baby. My baby got released the day before and my mother and sister took her home. I pleaded to get out of the hospital to see her and they eventually let me go 2 days later with a heart monitor attached under my shirt, accompanied with a tape recorder type machine clipped to my waist. I almost died giving birth. I didn't know how to love this child but she taught me how by loving me. I was her hero and I would do anything in the world to take care of her. I didn't matter, I lived for her. At this point I was just an object wanting to be loved. Wanting someone to help me take care of my baby.

I ended up with three more children by 22 by a homeless hood, ghetto dude named Ronald. Ronald was nice at first until I let him move in after I got pregnant with our second child. I had a small apartment my father's friend owned. I was only 16 when I moved on my own. At that time crack had taken over our small city and out of towners brought more drugs in. Everybody starting smoking crack, walking around like zombies. It took most of our parents but I was fortunate to get both my parents back from that terminal disease.

Ronald was my first bid with cheating. I kept quiet and let him do him. He had a bad temper and I didn't know how to fight so I avoided them especially with him.

Ronald starting making money and was feeling himself. He bought an ole school car and pimped it out. He would stop by frequently to get more drugs and slept there most of the time. I guess that qualified him as my boyfriend in my mind. I start getting jealous and feeling insecure. Everybody was telling me he was cheating and we argued all the time. He used to pull up with this chick barely old enough to drive said he let her drive him around cause she had a license. I later found out he was paying her mother crack to sleep with her. We were back and forth and after I gave birth to our son, my fourth child, we were at a low point. My mother wanted me to stay with her because after I gave birth, I was getting my tubes tied. Ronald was mad I was leaving three days after I gave birth and had surgery. He kicked me in my stomach and my butt hit the metal heat vent. Blood start pouring out of my vagina. My mother showed up and pistol whipped Ronald until he could barely stand. I stayed so she didn't get involved after that. He provided everything and would throw it in my face and any money I made went to him. I lost my voice. I lost me. I wasn't a factor. It was all about everybody else. I hated him. I prayed God would take him away because I couldn't. I felt stuck. I would take myself to a different place mentally when he would hit me. I would imagine a bag or a box entering and would place him in it and imagine the object taking him away. My only defense was prayer and meditating. I was so weak inside I didn't defend myself, it was pitiful.

CHAPTER 3

A young woman I am with a daughter half my age
same life I lived phase after phase
I pray to god please forgive my sins
I don't want my lil girl in the same life I'm in
I try really hard I always do my best
to find out my daughter is already having sex
I say a lot of stuff I get loose with my words
I want them to be much better I want them to learn
I pray to you god please tell me what to do
I pray to you god please it can only be you
I lied my bed I'm paying the price
I've learned my lesson I can't go through it twice
this cycle continues year after year
my mother her mother her mother shed the same tears
now I'm going back in time when I was a lil girl
would never expect this much of this cold, cold world
now she's been caught it's all my fault
the difference between us she's already been taught
I love her to death she's already left I surrender
I'll give you my very last breath.

Dangerously In Love: Blame it on the Streets

Raising a child being a child is impossible. The only thing you can teach them is what you know, so it's important to be what you expect them to be. By the age of 22 I had four kids, and had moved about seven times until I landed a low income job. I dropped out of school in the eleventh grade but managed to take my GED the following year and went on to be a medical assistant. I really didn't have faith in being a medical assistant, all I knew was I had to keep going. I had to do something. As I grew into a woman, I started to get a little more attention and had boyfriend after boyfriend always thinking they going to save me but they didn't. It was always worst, and in the meantime my daughters watched as I sought attention from the comfort of a guy. I hated myself. Life was hard, I had to feed, clothe, and provide shelter for four children. I shut down emotionally and started drinking, smoking weed, and selling weed. I did whatever it took to make me feel better and I couldn't fail. These kids deserve everything and just because I was young didn't mean they wasn't going to get it.

While I was selling weed and partying feeling myself, Fat Albert turned into a beautiful, black, curvy woman. I'd landed a top drug dealer from outta town who I thought treated me like a queen. I was his main chick in my city but he had a girl where he lived. I had access to all the boosters, food stamps, furniture and cars. Me and my children were on top of the world. He moved me outta low income housing and I finished school comfortably. Tony had spent time in prison, ironically with my father and they were connected in the line of work.

They did a lot of business together and my father was cool with him for business purposes but he didn't want me with him. Even with all the damaged I allow to happen to myself, I was still his baby girl and he wanted to protect me.

One night on one of our frequent outings to the "room" we stopped at a party store. Tony told me when we first started dating he got set up and attacked by some junkies he knew. He used to live at their house when he would come to town and they would let him conduct business from there. One night while he was sleeping, the couple attacked him with knives and bats. They beat him to a pulp and he escaped but endured a year in a coma and 78 stab wounds to his body including 206 stitches. Five years had passed since that happen and never in a million years would I have thought we would bump into the guy at the party store that night. Tony told our driver to go back around the corner. There was a guy on the pay phone and you couldn't see his face. The driver parked and Tony got out the car and walked in the over ten feet of snow to the payphone. I could hear his feet crunch as he walked slowly up. Once Tony got within arm's reach of the man, he called out his name. He turned around and instantly Tony grabbed his throat and slung him to the ground like a rag doll. There was terror in his eyes and you could tell he remembered who Tony was. Tony turned into a monster and beat him and drug him through the white snow causing it to turn red all around him. Tony beat him until his body went limp.

I froze, I was shaking so hard. The driver screamed for Tony to get back in the car. Tony turned around to reply and the guy got away. Tony was a big guy so he wasn't going to chase after him. The man started yelling call the police and Tony got in the car. We drove off. That night at the room while Tony was showering and washing off the blood. I got on my knees and prayed. I wasn't equipped for this, it felt like I was living someone else's life. I was far from gangster. I never had a fight in my life.

I continued to date him and tried to forget about that night. I was paranoid about the police kicking in the door. My house was full of drugs. People were coming in and out my house and all I could think about is when I was in that raid as a child. Those dogs. I didn't want my home raided. I didn't want to go through that. Fortunately for me, Tony got caught on the highway with two bricks and seven pounds of weed. He went back to jail and I was back to my low income lifestyle.

I started hopping from boyfriend to boyfriend again. In the meantime my daughters were well aware as young ladies themselves what I was about. I guess you could say I was 'sac chasing', selling myself to the highest bidder. Everything was about money so to say. I never prostituted or tricked. I just chose a certain class of men. While I should have focusing more on teaching them to be ladies, they were watching me and followed suit. My fifteen year old ran away. Word on the street she was trying to get my house robbed because she thought I was holding drugs for dudes. My mother finally forced me to find her and when I did, she was pregnant. I had to make some changes.

Aletta H.

Broke

I cannot break I pray to you Lord
Deeper in faith, with my shield and my sword
Train me to endure when my weapons are down
Lead me thru darkness to higher ground
Lead me back fast when I go astray
Take me so far I don't remember the way
My soul full of holes that open and close
Constant reminders of older lessons been told
From the worst pain felt to the times of pure enjoyment
I'm your child my father forever keep me anointed
I know I'm not perfect and I make plenty mistakes
I pray to you lord I cannot break I cannot break

I started working at the factory only because it was a dollar more than what I was making as a medical assistant. It wasn't enough. I was not making it at all. I started braiding hair after work to supplement my income. I was exhausted. With a baby coming I didn't know what to do and my daughter was clueless. I still sent her to her room. Our relation was forced because she didn't want to be there and I didn't want her there. She would try to run away and my nephew Ant would come dragging her back in. I stayed to myself for the most part. I'd vowed to stay single and focus on my kids. I had to get my relationship with my children better.

My sister stopped by one day and gave me her old computer and a printer she had gotten at a second hand store. She had knew how I loved to write and was trying lift my spirits. I was grateful for it. I thought I was in heaven. I had a chance to spill my guts on paper, in words. I had my place of comfort back where I could drift away and let the words flow like I was speaking in tongues. I was figuring out my life through my own words and I needed that. I also made money blogging. I started writing poems, making flyers, birthday cards, photos, business cards and checks. I just dabbled a little at first to see how the check would look. I was good. I had a couple friends I showed. They wanted one, so I sold them a $500 check for $100. That was the quickest money I'd ever made but I was scared to death of jail. I only did it enough to get what I needed.

My kid's father stopped by on a hum bug. He was yelling because he heard what I was doing with the checks. He was mad I didn't cut him in and was searching for my purse.

I had always hid my purse because I thought the kids were stealing from me. He stormed through the house knocking everything over. I didn't react because the last thing I needed was to get kicked out my low income home. By this time I knew I had spectators because of the chaos. The kids went to their room, they knew the routine. As I watched my kids go upstairs I knew what would happen as soon as they were out of sight. I felt a quick rush of air and saliva hit my face accompanied by a bitch slap so hard I saw stars. I didn't fight back. I was too scared. I wasn't a fighter. I begged him to stop but he only feeds off of my weakness and continued to go even harder.

Ronald grabbed my head and slammed it into the front door. I almost lose consciousness. Ronald kicked me in my stomach so hard I flew into the closet and the door shut. I grab the knob to keep him from getting in but he was so much stronger than I was and snatched it open anyway. I balled up and shielded my face. He walked over and swung his fist fiercely at my body. I couldn't take it anymore, so I jumped up and grabbed Ronald's face with my nails. He grabbed my throat and his hands were so tight around my throat, I tasted blood. I prayed the police would come or God would just take me. The emotional scars were way worst then the physical scars. The little fight I had in me was easily took.

Am I cursed with pain
loose with my words?
In vain
Am I selfish
I love me?
Back and forth going insane
are my expectations
Too high
should I let bygones?
Go by
should I ignore
My intuition
live my only life
A lie
I can't settle
For stuff
I love too hard
Too much
a shallow stepping stone
Mentally pulling me back
a false interpretation of love
Trying to throw me off track
I'll never forget
All the loves that I had
I found a part of me
some of it good
Some of it bad
I'll pray tonight to heal me

Aletta H.

Make me feel none of that empty pain
I'll pray tonight to not to feel
Bad about myself I
Wasn't to blame
I'll ask god to help me
Get further in life
do what's right
hug my kids
When it's time
To say good night
I'll pray for my lost love
To get blessed get healed
I'll pray my lost love
Won't feel this pain
That I feel
oh Lord please
Forgive me for my sins
I can't do this
Not again, not again

I didn't want to fight, I didn't have fight in me. I wanted it to be over. I was broken my spirit, my existence, my mind, and my thoughts. I was broken. I was trying and getting nowhere, but I was trying. The police arrived and I was screaming.

"He took my money, that's for my bills and to get grocery."

"You can take him to small claims court." The officer replied.

"What about my kids? They have to eat!" I cried.

Just before they cuffed him, he threw a ten dollar bill at me and smiled. I felt myself go to another place. I snatched my leather spiked belt off and lashed him across the face and blacked out. I was screaming and fighting. I had so much rage inside of me that I didn't care what happened. I couldn't take that blow to my pride. The police rushed me, throwing me to the ground and put me in handcuffs. I had shut down and I let them put me in cuffs and cried. I also went to jail for aggravated assault. Because he lost sight in his left eye, he only got a slap on the wrist.

I got out the next day on a personal bond because I didn't have a record. When I arrived home, it was to an eviction notice on the door and I didn't have a penny to my name. I cleaned my house and made the kids noodles. I had only enough food for about a day if I stretched it. I could barely walk. My head was banging and I was scared to death. I didn't know how I was going to feed my kids. I sat down at the table and made myself a check for $10,000.

I felt like a zombie that day. I went upstairs and got dressed in some casual attire. I put makeup on and caught the city bus downtown. Which was two blocks from the bank. I walked in the bank as calm as I had ever been in my life. I smiled and conversed with the teller. I had to wait for the manager's approval. I made me a cup of complimentary coffee and had a seat. I wasn't worried at all as the teller smiled and motion me to the counter. She counted out $10,000 in hundred dollar bills and put them in an envelope. I walked to the nearest store and caught a cab to McDonald's and then home.

When I got home I had the kids pack and I moved two days later. I paid my rent for a year, bought a hooptie and furnished our home and I tried to forget what I did, but it haunted me daily. It was almost a relief to see the US Marshall at the door 4 months later. I just wanted to get it over with. I ended up spending one hundred and four weekends in jail and being placed on five years federal probation.

Dangerously In Love: Blame it on the Streets

Right after it's over give yourself a little time
You'll find yourself accepting the first one in line
Go thru your emotions only you can find what's lost
Put your guards up so you can clearly detect false
Even when you think him everything he was not
Remember the things important don't settle thinking
that's all you got
Take that love that you took back
Life isn't fiction live it in fact
Love yourself like no one else can
Don't sacrifice yourself for the attention of a man
Do your thang be everything god made you to be?
Follow your dreams be on the receiving side, this time
with your love so deep
"Thirst is a curse that makes lonely feel worst"
Take your time remember your self-worth
Don't forget always give yourself some time
You'll end up filling that space with the first one in line.

Aletta H.

I had two months left of my rent and I needed sum cash. I needed to be saved, I needed that false security that I got from a man. I was drinking and smoking weed until I went numb. While playing a friendly game of spades with my friend Rhonda and her guy at the time, I met his friend Justin. Justin was a white guy and I wasn't into to white guys so it wasn't a big deal but I noticed Justin kept flirting while we played. I really didn't think he would be attracted to me. I was still broke and vulnerable. He was really sweet, very handsome and we became friends. He would come over and we would talk for hours and he opened up about things and I did too.

Justin went to his parents to buy us a house. He knew my situation and I believed in him. Seven days before my next rent payment was due he gave me the keys to a 5 bedroom house a couple blocks away. It needed a little work but it was definitely ready to move in. Ironically, I lived in the house as a child and me and my sister's name was still carved in the closet. I was excited. He started repairing what needed to be fixed and by this time we were a serious couple. I loved him and he loved me. He was the type of white guy who acted blacker than a black guy. He started hanging out late, but I trusted him.

I was secure for the first time in my life. In return I would do anything to make him happy even if it was facing fears and phobias. He loved animals, cats, birds, snakes, but he had a special love for pit bulls. Even though I was scared to death, I let him raise two in our basement. He put extra reinforcement on the door so I was comfortable.

I would try to feed them through a small slot, I would talk to them and they would respond. I got comfortable enough to pet them through the gate but that was it. By me getting comfortable with the dogs, it led to more pets. He purchased a fish tank that covered our whole bedroom wall that housed an alligator and a crocodile, which I hated. Their eyes would glow at night and give me nightmares but I dealt with it. He showed up one day with a small white kitten with a small grey spot on her back. She looked like a toy I held her in my shaking hands and she balled up scared of me. I treated her like my child and she grew into a beautiful intelligent cat. My family and friends couldn't believe I had a pet and neither could I.

Things started to alter our relationship. Justin liked to do things like go out with his friends shooting in the woods drunk. He came home one night panicking. He and his buddies would street fight in a makeshift ring and he broke someone's neck and paralyzed him. The dude end up being only 17 so the police was at my house everyday looking for him. He starting drinking a lot and we grew further apart. He started to get in to trouble with the law for dog fighting and getting into altercations with everyone about them. I moved out. I felt we were all at risk there because the house was packed with guns.

After living in that house for 2 years, I found myself back in an apartment. I left a lot of things but I took MY CAT. Justin started calling and stopping by my apartment drunk and out of control. I ended up getting a restraining order against him but that piece of paper didn't protect me.

Aletta H.

I had just returned from work one day and noticed a big red stain leading up to my porch and I panicked. I was scared to go any further to see what it could be. I started yelling and my neighbor came out and escorted me away while his son went to see what it was. As soon as he reached the porch. I heard a shallow meow. I ran to the porch and my beautiful cat, my friend, my baby was lying there mangled. All four of her paws were out of place, they had been broken. There was blood all over her pure white fur and a look of terror in her eyes. There was feces coming out of her as her body seized up and released. My heart was broken. Tears poured down my face as I stared at my baby. The neighbor put her in a basket and called the Humane Society to pick her up they put her to sleep immediately. She was dying slowly and they took her out her misery. Justin called all night taunting me about the cat. I knew he did it. His wallet was on my porch with blood on it. Justin had made threats before but I didn't believe he would do it, he loved animals. He told me he had grabbed her by her back and front legs and jerked them until they all broke. I was scared of him but Justin eventually ended up with another black girl. He eventually got arrested for shooting his friend while they were drunk at a club and ended up doing life in prison. Luckily, I didn't catch that bullet.

CHAPTER 4

Wanting to be loved,
Wanting to belong,
Wanting to experience the passion in love songs,
Even if it's wrong
Daddies' lil girl,
Swallowed by the world,
Knight in shining armor costume
Subliminal messages
Like odorless fume
Everything is doomed
Her beauty inside
Outside shy's
Which forces her beauty to hide
Wounds wide open unattended
Open for infection
Heart prone to rejection
Fast paced in the wrong direction
Need direction,
No faith,
Lost in the same place
Weakness isn't fate.
*After so many times of bumping your head against the
wall*
You may have slipped but eventually you will fall

Aletta H.

I was content for a while working, scraping up money for everything. I didn't go anywhere but work and home. It was hard physically and emotionally taking care of my family but I did it. My parents were getting older. I spent a lot of time with them. I needed their guidance. I needed to start over and listen to them and be a better person for my children. Through everything I always turned to them. My parents were always the final say. My father's word was bond. My father was proud of me. He could see me growing and we became close again. I would take him to his chemo when he was unable to drive. We would laugh the whole time. He would be impressed when I interacted with the nurses and doctors and could understand and translate it to him.

My sister had gave her life to God and asked me to attend church with her one day. I had to come out of my shell and interact again. I came to a place inside where I was afraid of outside. I went to work, home and my parents. I didn't know at the time that I was feeding an anxiety disorder that I've always had unnoticed. The fears from out of nowhere of dogs grew into a fear of most things, even people. I had thoughts running through my mind constantly that something bad was about to happen. I had to open up about the raid when I was a child. Something stuck that night. Something that night placed a fear of unexpected occurrences in me that I couldn't let go. It effected my life; that fear from nowhere.

That night haunted me, the loud voices, the dogs
barking, all that I blocked out. I was too young to handle
that situation and stored it till now. I never processed it.
It was stirring and I needed help. I needed spiritual help.
I needed council. I agreed and went to church with my
sister. I was nervous but I didn't turn back. She picked
me up and we went. It was beautiful, as soon as I walked
through the doors I felt calm, at ease. I had thoughts
running through my mind prosecuting the bad thoughts.
I realized it wasn't my past that fed into my anxiousness.
My anxiousness was a choice I made from the life I
chose to live. I was getting answers through the preacher
and the songs. The words of the preacher flowed through
the room like it was meant for me. I was ashamed of
myself. I needed to hear his message. The choir sang. I
could feel it in my heart. My body released and let the
words from the songs dance for me and sway through my
whole being. I could feel something easing my soul.
Something opening up. I was so damaged. I didn't know
where to go. I just knew I should be there at that moment.
The words were meant for me to hear, *Now behold the
Lamb*. I cried so hard and took it all in. *The precious
Lamb of God*, I went to the front when it was time to get
prayed for. The help I needed man couldn't give me. I
needed a higher power. I needed to be saved from all my
sins. I cried so hard and took it all in.

I wasn't scared in that room packed with people
watching me walk down the aisle to marry my fate. I
wasn't shaking. I didn't freeze. I was calm. I reached the
front and man and a woman approached me. My eyes
were pouring out the pain and had a long way to go.
They placed their hands on my head and shoulder and
started to pray.

Aletta H.

I closed my eyes and there words turned to mumbles. I felt a fullness overcome me. I started mumbling with them but did not fully understand what was happening to me. They walked me to a small pool, and place small cap on my hair and a white shawl over me. The pastor came up and hugged me. He put his hand in mine. It was like I already knew I was ready. He prayed over me and I heard horns in my ear. The sound got louder till everything went blank. My soul was claimed. I was saved. I understood and believed everything was going to be better for me. I had faith that the prior lessons were to avail and to get me to a better place. I had direction, I knew what I had to do. I had to give myself to God. I had to live by the rules of Him. In return, He would provide my every need.

I changed. I would work and go home and pray. Teach my kids prayers. It was amazing my needs were furnished miraculously. We didn't have much my landlord came to me and showed me the storage unit under our apartment building. She said whatever I needed, I could have. There was dishes, comforters, books, a TYPEWRITER, clothes that fit my children still new with tags on them like it was meant for me, a gift from God. He showed me He could provide for my family and I believed Him. I was still lonely inside. I wanted a husband, a mate, someone to love me like I loved my children. When you develop a constant relationship with God, He answers your prayers. You got to watch what you pray for. I prayed for a husband daily. A husband who would marry me, we would grow old together and live happily ever after.

Dangerously In Love: Blame it on the Streets

The devil is so busy
When you're doing what's right in life
He takes your weaknesses
Camouflage them with a false light
Everything given is not a blessing,
Put forth in front to provide a lesson
Sometime when we surrender,
We are selling our soul
As bright as it shines,
Everything that shines is not gold
Life can be hard
We all want to be saved
Think everything over
Make sure you're not digging Ur own grave
I'm so tired
What's wrong with me?
I'm so lonely inside
An empty space
A need not to be denied

Aletta H.

I felt so beat up working in factories and taking care of four kids. I finally got accepted for section 8, so my rent was only $112 a month. I had a little breathing room but not much. I was at a low point. I felt like a zombie. I was tired. I started to go to clubs on the weekends with my friends. I was shy, insecure and I couldn't dance. I mean even if I wanted to, I was so uptight I couldn't move. So much had occurred it was hard for me to relax. I let anxiety take over most of my life. I was a nervous wreck most of the time. I got a little liquid courage when I was drinking though. My birthday was coming and I and my friends planned a special night out. We went shopping and they picked out a short blue jean skirt and a hot pink ruffle top with pink stilettos for me to wear. I was looking and feeling good. I didn't get the courage to dance but I mingled. I bumped into a guy from our neighborhood whose birthday was that day also. We chatted up a storm. I knew what type of guy he was from jump. He worked in the street.

Jimmy had about six baby mamas and 3 maybe babies. I didn't take him serious. He would stop by and bring flowers, food, and candy. He was trying hard but everybody I knew told me he was bad news. I used to put a chair besides my bed for him when he was over late I refused to sleep with him. Jimmy and I were good friends and we did a lot of things together. We went to concerts, plays, and comedy shows. It was great but I had my guard up. After about a year of being friends, our birthday was coming back around and we decided to throw a party at my house. He supplied everything. My house was packed with family and friends. I was nervous about the amount of people that was there because there was a lot of people I didn't know.

I walked on the porch with my friend Sonya. I was telling her how uncomfortable I was with the amount of people. I didn't know any of those thugs. We laughed and shared a cigarette. As we were about to go in, Jimmy came out and planted a big kiss on my lips and wished me a happy birthday. I couldn't deny I was feeling him. He helped me a lot and made life so much easier for me. As we were about to walk back in two guys were walking up.

"Who is that?" I asked in frustration

"You tryna holler at them niggas?" Jimmy asked with a coldness in his eyes.

"You can't be serious." I laughed.

Jimmy grabbed me by my brand new micro braids and yanked me to my knees. I could hear braids rip from my scalp. He grabbed them tighter. Jimmy drug me by my hair back in the house to the party. Everybody was screaming at him to chill and let me go. My friend Sonya instantly start punching him everywhere telling him to let my hair go. He refused. Sonya was from Chicago, she wasn't for no games she always ready for war. Sonya drew her fist back and hit him hard in his face and he almost fell. All the while my hair was still intertwined in his fist. He yanked up and snatched my hair out.

I jumped up and ran to the bathroom. I looked in the mirror and over a third of the left side of my hair was gone. There was nothing but red scalp. I screamed and people were coming in trying to calm me down. I wanted to block it all out. I was going to take myself out. I had a plan. I wanted it over.

As I screamed profanity and cried the party had broken up. There were still a couple people trying to control the situation. One of his friends rushed him out of the house scared the police was going to come. Everybody left. I stood there shaking and crying, I just wanted it over. I thought of how I was going to die and rambled through the house. I was too scary to do something painful so I took a bottle of pain pills and went to sleep. That was it. I had made my mind up. I couldn't live this life anymore.

I went to sleep fast because of the liquor I had been drinking. I woke up a few hours later vomiting and shivering. I threw up so much I was dry heaving for hours after. My head was banging and my body was weak from vomiting. I started praying, crying, begging God for help. I slept most of the next couple of days. My name was buzzing in my little town. I was ashamed to go outside. Jimmy was sending flowers and gifts. He had people stopping by bringing food to the kids and trying to get back in with me. I was broken again. Jimmy said he was scared someone would take me from him and sobbed to me apologetically. I forgave him bald headed and all. The only thing I thought of was my children. I wanted them to have everything they needed.

I felt like I sold my soul to the devil. Jimmy could be the nicest man I knew and then he would turn into a monster. His insecurities kept him in other women's faces. He didn't have any limits to the girls he was trying to sleep with. For some reason he was attracted to things he shouldn't have. Like his friends wives and girlfriends. I think it gave him a feeling that he was better than them. I tried to sweep his behavior under the rug cause he would deny it then pacify me with a gift.

It was nice to have Gucci handbags, jewelry and expensive clothes. I was kept. I didn't have to work as long as I stayed in the house, cooked, and cleaned. Jimmy paid everything. He filled my section 8 home with flat screens and new furniture. It was like he was my father. He took care of me and mine to the fullest. I learned to just be quiet and not complain about the other women.

I kept so quiet I lost my voice. I didn't have an opinion. I didn't have a say about anything. I was like a maid to him and would serve his food in bed, wash and iron his clothes. He even had me lining him up and not knowing how scared I would mess up and get slapped. I forgot what I liked to watch on TV, what I liked to eat or wear. I was just a shell of myself and only what Jimmy wanted me to be, which was still not enough. I tried writing Jimmy letters explaining how I felt and he would turn it around and just say that I was complaining. It was a privilege to have him, somebody to pay my bills. Jimmy continued to cheat through our whole relationship. Jimmy wanted to move to a better neighborhood and get me farther away from my friends and family so I was unreachable. I switched my section 8 across town and we moved to the suburbs.

CHAPTER 5

He loves me so what if he cheats
That comes along with being in the street
So what he doesn't respect me
Beats me,
Feelings broke silently
I can't say a word
He is always right
When I open my mouth
It turns into a fight
I can't do all this alone
I've been a mother
Before I was grown
Deep down I know I'm worth more,
Having kids doesn't make me a whore
I'm beautiful,
Intelligent
My spirit is just torn
There's more in store
I'm finally wanted
My family is complete,
It's all about the whole
It's not about me
I don't want for nothing material things that is,
I need the security it all about my kids
Sold my soul to the devil
Signed on the dotted line,
Nothing left
Pretending that I'm fine
Years have passed
I'm still here
Living my life
In constant fear.

It was nice to show my children a different scene. They changed schools. We were finally out of the hood. Even though I hated life I could show them there was more in life. Our new house was gorgeous. We put leather furniture and bedroom sets in every room. I led the household cleaning and cooking and making sure everybody was on point, even Jimmy. I would tell him things about people he was hanging out with. It would come to pass. He told me early in the relationship he didn't know how to love he just knew how to provide. He had self-esteem issues even though I thought he was the shit. He played himself with girls who weren't even worth his time but just wanted some money. I found out early he was paying bum bitches for sex. He would even give them heroine or crack cocaine. All that was over my head. The only drug I indulged in was weed. I see what happen to people when they got hooked on drugs I was bad enough. I wouldn't even try. I blocked all that out.

One night he passed out drunk and I went through his phone I found a picture of a dark skinned girl bent over showing her camel toe from the back. She had to be 500lbs. I thought it was a joke. I went back in and found conversations back and forth. I was hurt. I tried waking him up but couldn't. I kept shaking his body and slapping his face. He finally got up after several slaps. He woke up and grabbed me but I managed to get out of his grip.

"Fuck your nasty ass, I'm done! You messing with bums, monsters, and losers." I shouted.

I didn't know how to feel. I almost rather that they be pretty or educated but they weren't. Jimmy was drunk. His eyes were blood shot red. He couldn't even comprehend what I was saying.

Aletta H.

While I'm yelling at him about the ugly bum crack head bitch, he balled his fist and punched me in the mouth. Blood slung across the room. I screamed and ran to the bathroom. He followed me.

"Oh yeah bitch, you talking shit?" He yelled.

I don't think this nigga was woke. He grabbed my arms before I close the door and yanked me back out. We were right above the steps and he slapped me. I kick him in the stomach, sending him back down the steps. I ran down the steps where Jimmy lay, barely conscious. I called the police. They came looking at me like I wasn't shit and tried to question me. I could barely talk. My whole top lip was blown out. The police called the ambulance but swept it under the rug. After that I knew I was on my own. I kept quiet. How could I compete with monster chicks looking like men? I couldn't.

I was still daddy's girl inside. I knew I was special. I ended up as a grown woman with my mother's figure, big butt small waist and a face pretty as a picture. I didn't feel pretty though. Every other day I was finding out about a different crack head bitch Jimmy was sleeping with and it made me feel worse. I needed to know why he was doing it. One day my daughter was getting a tattoo by Bigems. He had her come to his friend's house. The whole time his friend kept talking about Jimmy and how good he was, how he spoiled her with drinks and weed. This girl was 400 lbs. with a severe case of acne and closely resembled a man. I wanted out because it seemed as if he didn't have any standards. I didn't know how to compete with monsters.

During this time my nephew was with me a lot. He had been diagnosed with Hodgkin's disease at 21 and was now 26. Ant was my oldest sister's son. She was ten years older than me she was like my second mother. She would have me all the time when I was a little girl. She moved out and had children when she was young. My sister was blessed to marry her high school sweetheart. He had always been my brother since then. My sister and I have always been close and her kids felt like best friends to me. We hung around each other. My sister was always there for me and my kids, so it broke our heart when he first got sick.

Ant was quiet. He loved to play basketball and he was fine, he resembled Dwayne Wade but finer. Ant was the complexion of a dark Arab. He had dark curly hair, not those tight curls but big curls with light brown eyes and a baby face. All my friends flirted with him. He was a ladies man but stayed faithful when he was in a relationship. He was going back and forth with treatment but was getting worst. He came to my house and stayed all the time. This time he was sick. He was small and he looked weak. We sat talking half the night laughing. My children loved my nephew Ant to death. They rearranged the rooms so he could have his own room and would take him food and water whatever he wanted. We took care of him while he was with us.

A couple days had passed. I noticed he wasn't leaving the room. I went to check in on him. He was lying there limp. He was exhausted. He was small and his eyes looked bugged from the weight loss in his face. I had to call my sister to come get him and take him to the doctor.

Aletta H.

That doctor visit ended up with a permanent stay in the hospital, on life support. I went up to the hospital to see him he had quickly declined. He couldn't speak. He reached his hand out to me when I was then and I would sit on the bed and hold his hand. I thanked him for being a big brother to my children and for being a role model to my son. I tried to staying positive and think that he would get better but I got a call a couple of days later to come to the hospital. They were taking him off life support to die. That was a pain I've never felt. What did they mean gone? What did they mean die? Not my nephew my sisters son.

I walked in his room surprised that he was still awake. Ant put his hand out for me to grab it in a room full of people. Even though no words were spoken, I knew exactly what he was saying. He knew I loved him and that he loved me. I walked down the hall to the waiting room when they took him off life support. I didn't want to see him die. I waited a couple minutes and returned to his room. I needed to be there for my oldest sister since she had always been there for me, she was my second mom. My sister, her husband and the remainder of their children were overwhelmed with tears, standing in a huddle crying. I could hardly breathe. You could hear a beep coming every so often and then a sound stating that it was over. The room was packed with tears. The doctor cried and balled in a fetal position; he loved him too. Nurses came in and fell to the floor crying. It was a horrific scene. For somebody who just began life to die. It was hard.

Jimmy in the meantime was still paying the big chick for sex. I blocked it out. My family needed me, they were more important. Our hearts physically hurt. We had to bury my nephew and none of us was prepared for it. It made me realize that the pain I allow is nothing compared to the pain beyond my control. We had Ant's funeral and tried to continue. Nothing was the same for my family after that. I realized that all the gifts in the world couldn't stop that kind of pain. I was growing through this. I was getting better. I didn't even know it. I started thinking about my life. I sacrificed my soul for financial stability. I still believed in Jimmy and wanted us to get better together. I loved him with all my damaged heart.

I really enjoyed all the stuff; all the fancy clothes, my SUV, my house. I took my role as woman of the house very seriously, making sure everything was clean and the kids and grandkid were fed and behaved. Jimmy was gone most of the time which I didn't mind. He was arrogant because of the status he had in the street. Jimmy got money and he paid for everything all the time. We threw all the holiday events at our house. He purchased tons of food for everyone and we would barbeque. I mean every holiday, every chance we could, we would have a barbeque with Jimmy on the grill and me in the kitchen making my side dishes. I can't say it was all bad. Jimmy loved the grandkids. We took them on as our own children financially while my daughter mothered them. We had couples that we were around a lot and my oldest sister (my second mom) and brother-n-law. It was nothing like the birthday/house party we threw when we first met. Jimmy was sweet. He showered me with hugs and kisses all the time.

He just didn't understand the faithful part of loving someone. I loved Jimmy more than I loved me. I kept my blinders on. I tricked myself mentally into believing that he wasn't cheating. Jimmy had a lot bottled up that he never addressed as a child. His issues came in many forms. His biggest issue was alcohol, especially dark liquor. His drink of choice was Hennessey. I swear every time I saw that bottle I was worried. I never knew if he was going to start crying like a vulnerable infant bout some petty things that he blew out of proportion or if he would believing somebody was trying to get over on him and get out of control. He would even get silly at times and have everybody laughing dancing and being the life of the party.

I wanted to get Jimmy out of the street. I took a serve safe class to open up a small restaurant. I found a location with everything already there, the dishes, tables, stove, refrigerator and cash registers. We just had to supply the food. Jimmy was worried we couldn't handle it on our own. He had his friend from back in the day go half with everything. I really didn't care for most of Jimmy's friends because they treated him like he was beneath them, even though he had more money than them. His friend Cle was cool. Cle was always polite. He had a more casual look to him. He was older. After some time of planning the restaurant together the three of us became close. Cle was like a brother to me. When I was down about the constant cheating he would jump down Jimmy's back. I respected the fact that he not once cut into me. He loved me like a sister.

After about a month of planning and advertising we decided that Cle and his staff would split the day with Jimmy and our staff, not knowing at the time that Cle and his staff were ex-convicts with serious crimes under their belt. Our staff consisted of two of my best friends and his brother in law. We opened up and everything went downhill from there. It's hard to put rats in suits and give them a business. It goes to their head. I became the weakest link although I started it. I got it legal advertised and did all the accounting. It was like it was me against them. I didn't even want to fight and Jimmy was on their side.

CHAPTER 6

My parent's health wasn't so well and they needed constant care. I shared the responsibility with my siblings. My mother had an earache and went in to urgent care and they found aneurysms in her brain which landed her in emergency surgery She was relocated to a bigger hospital about 40 miles away and had surgery immediately. It was hard. My mother had been so strong her whole life and endured the deepest pain you could imagine yet she maintained a classy kind of boogie, scars and all. After surgery snapped back quickly and checked herself out the hospital to help with my father. My father wasn't doing well but he kept a smile on his face. It was hard for him to walk. It got so bad he would have to use a cane and a crutch but have the nerves to drive and want me to ride with him. Of course I did it, I loved my father but I was scared to death. He was the greatest man I've ever known on earth. I would do anything for him and I tried to give him everything.

I would work my shift at the restaurant. We started getting complaints about the other shift they were slacking. Jimmy would come straight in go to the office and play computer games. I ran the whole shift. The spot was bringing in money. It got popular quick. I wasn't benefiting financially for all my time and effort to get it established. I wanted out, I was exhausted and everybody was getting rich but me. I think Jimmy liked to keep me needing him. He issued out cash to me but it wasn't the same. Jimmy was at a high point in his life. He had a business, the streets were treating him good. He could be somebody out there. He could "pretend" he was the man. All the chicks had their hand in his pockets.

They made him feel like he was the shit. Jimmy's intentions was to just fuck. He got a thrill out of sleeping with random chicks. You could say he like a variety of women and it was getting out of control.

I wanted out. I left the restaurant and Jimmy. I continued to help with my parents. Jimmy and Cle felt like I messed up the restaurant by leaving. I couldn't stand to be there. Chicks were coming in getting free food that I cooked. Jimmy treated me like crap around everyone in the restaurant, like he hated me. The other staff members would hit on me or swat my butt and he would pretend he didn't see. One night Jimmy didn't come home. I called up to the restaurant and asked Cle had he seen him. Cle and his friend came by my house instantly. They said I needed to leave Jimmy. He was cheating and lying about his money. They said they would give me a thousand dollars a week if I left him. I didn't get it. I thought Cle was his boy, his brother, my brother. Cle didn't say it insinuating he was trying to get with me. He just wanted it over between me and Jimmy. Cle and his friends always told me about all the things Jimmy was saying about me and my family, but I still didn't get it. I eventually realized that Cle was on the down low. It wasn't me he wanted, it was Jimmy. Cle told me about a prior night when Jimmy was drunk and out of control and I called Cle to come get him. Cle said Jimmy was faking to get out the house. Little did Cle know, Jimmy told me he woke up on an air mattress with Cle. I was dumbfounded. I definitely couldn't compete with a guy if it was true.

It was hard to be quiet because he was doing dirt and he put his guilt on me. I put him out the house and he left with no incident. Jimmy was free to do whatever he wanted, yet he called me and threatened me over the phone. I could hear Cle and his buddies in the background when he would call chanting ignorantly speaking Ebonics.

"Her mama half dead doe."

"Her pops legs barely can work."

The phone would hang up and I would be in tears. I couldn't believe Jimmy was allowing them to speak about my parents. He had told these thugs about the intimate things we talked about. I couldn't allow him back I had to get away. I'd always kept in contact with Tony and we were good friends, like family, at this point in life. I called him and he got me a train ticket later that day. I hadn't left the house in 5 years. I took care of home, I took care of my kids and grandkids, parents and Jimmy. It was foreign for me to board that train with a bag and go. As soon as I arrived at the train station, he was there smiling. Tony's mother was ill and he moved in and took care of her. We went to their house. She was lying in a neatly made bed with white covers, fancy sheets and curtains to match. Tony charged straight in her room.

"Hey Mama, remember that chick from Clarkston I've been telling you about forever my friend?" He gently asked her.

She gave him a look letting him know she was confused about who he was referring to.

"Mama show her your nails. I did them." Tony proceeded as he grabbed his mother's neatly manicured hand in different colored polishes. "That's that hood rat style Mama!" He laughed.

She still gave him an unknowing look. My heart went out to Tony, here he was the thug who had beat a man to a pulp, delicately painting his mother's nails and caring for her every need while she lay in a bed. I could see pain written all over his face as he smiled and continued.

While Tony went out to get dinner I unbraided his mother's cornrows and then braided them back up in a different style. I sat there and reflected on my life. I just didn't get it. I always did everything for everybody. I changed. I was a great person. I was hurt Jimmy would turn his back on me. I was scared for my father.

Tony returned and we had dinner. He played the funniest clips online. We laughed so hard my face was wet. I needed to laugh out loud, it felt well. I was tense. We slept on a couch watching clips laughing till three in the morning. Tony knew my visit had nothing to do with intimacy. I needed my friend and he provided that. I stayed for two days and returned back to reality.

Aletta H.

Anxious

Jumping out my skin
Living in sin
Nothing within
Fears
Tears
Wasting years
Unsure of now and before
Soul sore
Scared of nothing
Forget your something
So tense
Edgy
Terrors running through my mind
Everything you notice
Represent a bad sign
Anxious
Mentally trapped
Surroundings are spacious
No matter what
You're inside feels
Your body screams anxious
Emotional arraignment
Out of place

Displacement
Nervous
Startled
Shook
Spirit took
Never-ending book
Can't concentrate
Sanity at stake
Always early
Feeling late
No patience
Just anxious

I left my phone off for those days just to get some air from home. I turned it back on while I was on the train to prepare myself for the worst. I was nervous to face the fact my father was declining. I had the feeling all the time I would get a call that my father passed. I was so scared. Fear took over most of my life. Too much was going on all the time. I expected the worst. Luckily, none of those calls were in my messages. Jimmy left several threatening messages calling me every kind of whore and saying how I ruined everything and that I should have shut up and stayed. Cle and his posse left messages harassing me. I was scared. I had to go home with convicts threatening me. I tried to put that to the back of my mind and went to visit my parents.

My father lay in a hospital bed in the living room. At this time hospice nurses were in and out of the house. His face lit up when he saw me and mine did too. I sat on the couch next to his bed. He was worried, so he asked me what was going on. I proceeded to tell him about the problems I was having with Jimmy and his friend Cle. I was hurt that after all this time Jimmy would turn his back on me and take the side of his friend. I also told him about Cle trying to pay me to stay away, it was too much. I wasn't going back. My father said I needed some space. I needed to figure things out on my own. No one was ever good enough for me in my father's eyes but he cared for Jimmy. My father was the father Jimmy never had. Jimmy cared for him too. My father was hurt to see me go through such a breakup. He was so proud we started a business and warned us of bringing people in. I cried. I was vulnerable when it came to my father. So I wept and pleaded for answers. I couldn't take much more. Life was kicking my butt.

Dangerously In Love: Blame it on the Streets

I went home to an empty house, no kids, no
grandkids, and no man. As soon as I sat on the couch,
my phone start ringing. It was Jimmy going on about
how I was to blame for leaving and how I started
problems with him and the thugs. He thought I should
apologize and come back. I was furious. I wasn't doing
any of the above. I didn't care if I was flat broke. It
wasn't enough money or things on this earth that could
make me do that. All I know is I did nothing wrong. I
did everything I was told to do above and beyond.
Jimmy changed because his pockets got swollen and
treated me like a crack head. Everybody changed got
cocky. I wasn't equip to have any sort of altercation with
any of them. The calls repeated for a week. Jimmy had
checked into a hotel down the street from our home. The
kids and grandkids were home I try to act normal.
Cleaning cooking taking care of everyone. Jimmy would
have his cousin drop money off to me. Just enough to
keep my head above water he knew what he was doing. I
needed to maintain. We talked all night on the phone and
he said he hate the business. Everybody having problems
working together. I was right. The business got to his
head. He was sorry for letting all that go on and treating
me like crap. I can't go back. I can't keep selling myself
literally for stability. I had to do better. I had to do it on
my own. Walk blindly in faith. I had too.

Aletta H.

Lost Bitch

Always mad nothing even wrong,
Emotional torments,
I'm humming church songs
Always pointing the blame
 Tryna run game,
To hide the shame
 Nothing's changed
The closest ones get it worst,
 The most hurt
Treated like dirt,
 Never first,
Cause what's in your purse
Always after something
You shouldn't have,
 Backstabber,
 Liar,
 Spits on your grave
Type and laugh
Stability gone,
Brain dial is pointed to wrong,
Those lifestyles don't last long
Like a mouse thinks its king Kong
Pride taker
Confidence breaker,
Fake dream maker
Want to be rich
Lost bitch

CHAPTER 7

Dark Circles

*These dark circles around my eyes a remembrance of all
the cries, lies, tryna hide what's inside
This hand I've been dealt is so hard to play, don't know
how to play it cause I'm not into games
Always thinking that good will overcome all, walking in
faith, only to fall
Negative surrounds me while all the positive is inside,
going back n forth until all positive dies
Tryna keep it clean so clean nothings there, when I'm
rolling in the deep things seem equally fair
My grandmother always told me being nice was a curse,
my big open heart can endure so much hurt
I've paid for my past over and again, everyday reminders
of all of my past sins
Believing a higher power will always be by my
side, bumpy roads makes this ride a hard ride
Just need a chance to prove all the negative wrong, going
thru the steps please don't take too long
Taken my only life one day at a time, you can see right
thru me dark circles around my eyes*

Aletta H.

Just as things were about to get heated up when four masked men came rushing through the back door all brandishing big metal objects in their hands. Jimmy got up and rushed toward the masked men and I froze. I watch strikes to Jimmy's head and blood pouring down his face as he fought for his life and I couldn't move. One of the large masked men approach me and started to swing repeatedly at my head and body causing me to fall to the floor. With blood blinding me, I balled up into a fetal position and prepare to die. I heard footsteps and the door open. I remain still praying the blows to my body stop. Everything became completely silent.

One of my eyes was completely swollen shut, I wiped the other in an attempt to see what was going on. I notice that the front door was open and I could hear Jimmy yelling outside. I tried to stand but it was of no use. My hand was swollen and felt as if I was wearing a baseball mitt from trying to cover my face. My legs were unrecognizable and I couldn't feel any pain. I was scared to go outside so drug myself over to the couch and started digging for my phone in

Apparently the masked men ran out when they saw someone pull up at neighbors' and Jimmy ran outside for help. The adrenaline was pumping through my system like a freight train, I managed to somehow run up the stairs not knowing my leg was broken to check on my youngest daughter who was 14. I was relieved to see she was still asleep in bed and hadn't heard a thing. All my children either sleep walked, talked, or something to do with sleep, so it wasn't out of the ordinary for her to be still asleep. I screamed her name and she jumped up screaming after seeing blood pouring down my face.

Jimmy ran up the stairs behind me also blood pouring from his head we all were panicking. We all proceeded back down the stairs. I felt my leg give out half way down the stairs. I lifted it off the steps and hopped down and sat on the couch. I was trembling so hard my teeth were chattering.

I found my phone and called the police. Once the ambulance arrived and finally got us to the hospital I was relieved. After we were rushed into the emergency room, the police wanted to question me and Jimmy about what had happened but I had no answers to give them. The cast was put on my leg and they finished stitching my head which now had about fifteen zillions left. By the grace of God I didn't feel any pain, it was like I was carried the whole time. Jimmy had seventeen staples in his head and two missing teeth. I called my sister to come get us from the hospital and after she picked us up we got dropped off to a hotel. All I could think was how I am going to see my father at the hospice home tomorrow like this it will kill him.

I was paranoid sleeping at the hotel. My eyes and ears where wide awake. Listening to the creaks and cracks of the night. I sobbed still in shock of the prior events. Jimmy held me in his arms and wiped away the tears. Who was those masked men really? I needed to know. Deep down I knew it was Cle and his friends, but Jimmy didn't believe that. It wasn't a robbery, nothing was taken. I had new TVs in boxes and Jimmy had a pocket full of money but nothing was taken. I think Cle hired them to come kill us, he wanted Jimmy to himself.

I was scared of outside. Fear had finally set up permanent residence in my mind. I was shook. I had to get myself together to see my father. I got up that morning and showered. I got dressed and left the hotel with one crutch, wore a baseball hat and some Gucci sunglasses. Jimmy drove me to see my father. When I got to my father's room, I left the crutch outside the door and walked in slowly, smiling and greeting my siblings. Everybody stopped, turned and looked at me as a solitary tear escaped my eye. I wiped it away quickly.

"Hello everyone. Hi Daddy." I said with a pitiful smile on my face.

My family blamed Jimmy because of his lifestyle but I allowed it. My father looked at me with pain written all over his face. He knew something was wrong because of the sudden silence from everyone in the room. I had on sunglasses so he couldn't see any physical scars, or so I thought. My father reached up and grabbed my arm which had a gauze bandage taped on it. I was in so much pain, I couldn't keep up with covering them.

"What happened to your arm?" He said with a confused look on his face.

I couldn't lie to him. He could see right thru me.

"Someone broke in our house and attacked us, but we're fine." I said.

My father's face went blank, he was clinching his fist and his mouth began to ball up.

"I'm gonna kill them!" My father blurted out.

His eyes filled with tears as I took off my shades to wipe my eyes in an attempt to keep my tears from escaping. The room was silent. My siblings looked in awe as they watched my father weep. There was nothing he could do to save his little girl. I couldn't bear to stay and continue to bring him pain. I felt guilty for the tears that I had caused my father to cry. I left the room sobbing.

Jimmy picked me up and we returned to the hotel. I didn't want to go back home. There was blood stains in the carpet as a reminder of the spot I was prepared to die in. I couldn't bring myself to look at them. We decided to stay at the hotel for a while and look for another house. I felt so unsafe in this town. I always found myself staring in the face of tall men, wondering if they were the ones who came in my home that night to murder us.

My father was stable. He still was sick, but he was at a point where he wasn't rapidly declining so I decided to move to a nearby city just to be comfortable. It was a big change. I put my whole life in Jimmy's hands, taking a chance and moving there with no one but him to be there for me. I found an apartment by the local mall and an excellent school district. My two youngest children, who were 13 and 14 at the time, were the only ones to make the move with me. My oldest daughters stayed in our hometown with my grandchildren. I instantly started looking for employment since I didn't want Jimmy to be my only means of survival. I really wanted out of the relationship but didn't know how to leave.

His plan was to go back to our hometown during the day to "work" and he would return home to me every night. I didn't mind that plan at all because Jimmy wasn't easy to be around. He would take everything out on me, no matter what it was. I'd rather he stayed there a couple of days and came home and broke me off every so often, but that would never happen. He had to know my every move. Jimmy kept a tight hold on me. He made me feel like I was doing something wrong if I would go outside or have company over. He wanted me all to himself so he could control everything. I think he knew if I got loose from his grasp that I would run. I think I would of too.

I had gotten to the point that I was so used to him making all the decisions and had become blind to a lot of the mental and emotional abuse. I'd lost myself a long time ago and he just strung me along. I couldn't make any decisions for us, not even something so small as suggesting what we would have for dinner. If I did, he would go as far as to get something else even if I had already gone to the store and got the food.

I looked for a job for what seemed like forever and kept landing jobs at local retail shops that didn't pay much. I became friends with the mother of my daughter's friend and she owned a care home. I eventually started working for her. It felt good to be away from home and Jimmy. To feel safe to meet new people who didn't know what I had been through, who didn't know my sad past. I worked as many hours as I could with her and she paid decently. I saved up money for a trip we were taking for our upcoming birthday.

I couldn't wait to go even farther away and get some air, even if it was with Jimmy. We did have a lot of good times together. Everything wasn't all bad, but it felt like our relationship was cursed from jump, since our first birthday together.

Months had passed and it was the day before our birthday I was so excited. I was on my way to get my hair and nails done and my mother called me. She was tired she was spending every day and night with my father. Some days were good and some were bad. This day she called and said she needed a little break. I told her to go take a nice long bath and relax. I reminded her of what a great person she was for caring for him the way she did her whole life. She agreed and hung up. As I prepared for my trip to Chicago the phone rang. It was my mother again.

"Oh my God! They say he's shutting down, he's in a coma!" She said frantically.

My heart stopped. I called Jimmy who was already there and told him to go check on my dad. I called my cousin to come and get me and drive me there. This can't be happening, not on my birthday, not on our birthday. I arrived at the hospital and he was lying there in the bed. He was lying on his back and you could see he was breathing but he was so still.

"Can he hear me?" I asked the nurse.

"I don't know for sure sweetie but it's worth a try." She said in soothing voice.

Aletta H.

I walked up to my father, my king, my everything and prayed he could hear me.

"Hi Daddy." I said with as much cheer as I could get in my voice.

His face didn't flinch. The room started to fill with all of my siblings, my mother's children and my father's children from a previous marriage. We weren't that close because of my mother stealing their mother's husband. They were older than us and looked like their mother more than they looked like my father but you could tell they were his children. My father's sister was also there and I love her to pieces. She was about 3 years older than me. Obviously their father was a player and had a few kids later in life. Everybody said me and her looked like sisters I thought we did too. I could use her ID when I was younger. My aunt sat by me all night while we watched my father breathe. We watched people come in an out to see him transition. The doctors would come in periodically and take his pulse. They would start with his ankles and move up. Just to inform us that he was shutting down. I couldn't believe it. I didn't want my father to pass. I wasn't ready for the closest person to me in the world to leave. My protection, my everything, and especially not on my birthday.

"He's waiting for tomorrow, he wants you to know how special you are and leave his final message to you." My aunt said to me.

I didn't see it like that. I couldn't believe this was happening as the night grew close to morning me, my mother and my aunt talked the night away and we included my father in everything we talked about. We laughed and we cried. We reminisced about good times. I went to the car to smoke a cigarette with my aunt and have a small toast for my birthday, which felt like I was drinking water. There was just too much going on for me to even catch a buzz. As we walked back in, you could hear a raspy sound like someone had a horrible cold in their chest. Tears started to roll down my aunt's face and she sat me down before we got back in the room.

"They call that the death rattle. It's getting close, he is dying." She whimpered, trying to prepare me.

Tears filled my eyes but never breached my eyelids. My face was hot and my body was cold. I had a lump in my chest that hurt with every time I breathed.

Aletta H.

My heart is heavy different scenes running through my mind

I felt this coming I needed a little more time

Who's going to protect me my daddies no longer here

Who's going to hold me and wipe away these tears

You loved me so hard no one can take your place

I feel so alone in this world so unprotected, so unsafe
I'm angry, I'm sad daddy I didn't ever want you to leave

Walking around like a zombie, I wish this was make believe

Everybody say in time it will get better

I can't see that happening, my time is never

I just want to hear you laugh, I need your advice

I wish I had a magic wand so I could bring you back to life

I know I have to continue, Lord knows I need help

I must play this hand out, these are the card I've been dealt

We walked back in the room and it was loud like snoring in his chest the sound was horrific. I'll never forget it. It was past twelve so it was officially our birthday. Jimmy had spent most of the day with my oldest sister and her husband. It was still our birthday and I wanted him to have some fun, so they had drinks and food over there. He called after 12 to say he was coming to stay with me and my family, to wait up for him and I did. He got there reeking of liquor and staggering. I held my hand to my mouth signaling him to be quiet. I made room between me and my mother on a small let-out couch for him.

"Jimmy be quiet you smell like liquor and you're going to feel real stupid when you wake up cuddled up with my mom."

I got off the couch and looked over at my father. I didn't hear anything. The snoring was gone. He wasn't moving.

"Oh my God, no!" I cried.

I walked over to him and my aunt woke up and stood up and looked at me. We both check his pulse and it was not there. He looked different than he looked earlier. He looked at peace. He looked relaxed. He looked like he wasn't there, it was just a shell of who he was. She pushed the button for the nurse to come and as the nurse walked in the door my mother woke up. Terror was in her eyes. She was shaking.

Aletta H.

The nurse checked his pulse in several places and started unhooking the machines. She wrote down some stuff and called for further assistance. My mother's body fell to the side of the bed as she started weeping. She couldn't believe what was happening. Jimmy, still inebriated, started to sob. I called my oldest siblings and they came immediately. My brother, my brother-n-law and Jimmy stayed in the room as they cleaned him off and put him in the bag. Me and my sisters took my mother out and shielded her face from him coming out on a stretcher in a body bag.

"I want to go to the morgue, I need to make sure he's okay." My mother yelled

We all held her in our arms and huddled around her. Everything went still but fast at the same time. It was the morning of my birthday and my father just passed.

I checked into a hotel room there and took a shower. My head was beating from crying. I didn't want to face anyone. Everyone knew how close we were. I felt sorry for myself. I couldn't believe this happened to me. I got dressed and preceded to my mother's house which was packed with people. I was happy they were there for her, but I just wanted to go home and cry. I didn't want to do this. I wanted to go home and forget. Everybody was looking at me as if I were diseased. I took it. The other grandmother of my grandkids was there. She took me off to the side. I could barely breathe, I was just there. She went in her purse and pulled out a bottle of pills, valium. She counted out ten and handed them to me.

I knew what they did and I popped one in my mouth. I just wanted the pain to go away.

I sat down at my mother's house and drifted. Family members would come and hug me and look at me with sympathy or wanting to see what I was going through to gossip about. I was completely numb. I couldn't react. I just sat there. My siblings and I had to plan the funeral, luckily working in that factory, he had an insurance policy which paid for it. Everybody was looking at me to make the obituary. I didn't even want to imagine the funeral let alone make a program for it but I did. I went home and made his program. I even wrote a poem quoting what he said all the time. It was a nightmare. I wasn't in a place to do this. Too much had happened. This was so final; my father, my everything was dead, and he died on my birthday.

I woke up the next morning and took another valium as soon as I opened my eyes. Me and Jimmy got dressed and headed thirty minutes to our home town. I could barely talk when my phone rang.

"We got to talk, I'm going to keep it funky" I heard a raspy voice say when I answered.

"Who is this?" I replied.

"I have been turning tricks wit yo man for three years and my two year old daughter is his. He would give me heroine to sleep with him." The raspy female continued.

I was so zoned out I just laughed. She said who she was and I almost peed my pants. On the highway, on the way to my mother's home, with him driving and I was hearing this. Jimmy stared at me and asked who it was. I lied and said somebody asking about the funeral. Jimmy could tell I was lying because I had a smirk on my face, almost evil.

"No big deal your baby mama tea just called." I finally responded.

"That ain't my baby mama, she lying. I let her suck my dick, that's all." He started screaming.

I didn't reply, I didn't care. Actually, I didn't feel anything. The valium had taken full effect and my emotions were turned off. We continued in silence. We pulled up at my mother's where we all agreed to meet and drive up to the service together. My father wanted to be cremated. He didn't want people ogling over his body. He told me that a long time ago and we made sure of that. There was a big picture of him in the front of the church surrounded by flowers. I sat by my mother and held her as she wept. It was hard to hear the service. It was all so unreal. I was kind of glad he wasn't lying there in a casket. I would have passed out.

After the heart breaking songs were over and everybody was in tears. We all went to the basement of the church where a meal was being prepared. I was hugged and kissed by family members, some I didn't even know.

I could feel eyes were on my every move like everyone was waiting for me to break. I didn't. I smiled and conversed with family. I kept a close eye on my mother. My mother had been with my father forty six years of her life. She met my father when she was fifteen years old. All she knew was taking care of him. Ironically, they didn't marry until two months before his death. That certificate didn't certify their love for each other; that had already been set in stone, but I think he did it for her peace of mind. Life had to continue for us without my god. After the meal was served we all met back at my mother's.

With any family you always have that one trouble maker, miserable with her own life, type hater. My father's cousin Londa was our family shit starter. She started in on my mother saying he always loved his first wife but my sister, the Christian, put her in her place and quickly told her she could leave if she going to be talking stupid; today wasn't the day. Londa backed off my mother.

We were all sitting outside in the back yard. It was nice seeing my siblings. I loved all of them dearly even my half-siblings, anything to do with my dad I was for. Londa started in on her brother's girlfriend stating her brother didn't want her that he was gay and child protective service was at her house all the time. We had had enough of Londa's behavior. We walked Londa to the front of the house and my sister was giving her a ride home. Londa continue screaming at his brother's girlfriend. It took all of us to hold her back from Londa. Finally she got free and preceded to beat the brakes off Londa in the front yard. My grandson ran inside to tell my mother (he was always in somebody business).

My mother ran to the front window to see what was going on. We was scared she couldn't handle that much drama, she was vulnerable. To our surprise my mother busted out in laughter and yelled out cheering whoop that bitch's ass and continued to laugh as Londa got beat up in her driveway. Weave was everywhere.

My sister finally got Londa in her car and drove off. We all laughed the rest of the day. It knocked the edge off the prior event. Later that night when everyone went home. I went over my favorite aunt's house to have a drink with her and her husband. Jimmy came too. The whole time I put to the back off my mind the trick baby. I got drunk and everything came pouring out. I was crying about my father. Still in shock about him passing on my birthday and having a boyfriend that pays crack heads for sex and got a baby by one. I couldn't keep silent.

"Listen muthafucka you out here cheating on me and I gave you my life bitch! Nigga you fucking 500lb dope feen monsters and I'm home feeling like shit. I'm done! I don't give a fuck if I lose everything I have. I'm done! You ain't shit and you don't deserve me." I ranted.

"That's not my baby with your dumb ass always listening to folks." Jimmy said jumping up in my face.

I had did some research and that little girl looked just like him. That dope feen wasn't lying on him.

"Nigga you obviously don't care about my life, you fucking raw at least you could have worn a condom." I spat.

"Let her talk. Let her get it off her chest, her dad just died." My aunt said intervening on my behalf.

I pushed Jimmy off the porch knowing I had back up and he walked away. Jimmy picked me up a couple hours later and I didn't say a word. I had shut back down. When we returned home I was planning to throw his stuff out and figure everything out on my own. My phone rang on the way back to the room it was Tia again.

"I just want to say me and Jimmy had a talk earlier tonight, he stopped by. He was mad because I had our daughter laying on the floor but I'm glad he came. We have an understanding now." She snarled.

I hung up and hit Jimmy in the face with my phone while he was driving. Jimmy pulled over the car. I wasn't scared at all, I was ready. To my surprise Jimmy started crying.

"I'm sorry, I'm sorry!" He pleaded.

"Sorry for what Jimmy? Sorry for fucking monsters?" I questioned.

Jimmy's head was down and he didn't reply.

"So you telling me you into 500lb dope feen monsters?" I questioned again.

"Yes." Jimmy said softly as he looked up at me.

He started the car back up and we drove to the room. I slept in the extra bed and cried so hard my eyes were swollen like golf balls. I hated my life. I didn't know what to do. All I knew was I had to get myself together. I had to get a job and wean myself off of Jimmy's money. The following weeks I looked hard for a job. I was applying for jobs I knew I didn't qualify for. I was book smart so I knew I could learn anything. I finally got a call one day to work at a doctor's office at the front desk. I went to the interview confident. I kept telling myself I had it. I meditated on how it would feel to work there. I envisioned myself getting up for work, putting on scrubs and paying my own bills, taking care of my own family. I started to act as if it already happened. I was practicing the law of attraction. I had read a lot about it and I believed it. I believed I could manifest anything I wanted in my life.

In the meantime, I barely talked to Jimmy. I had an exit plan or so I thought. Jimmy started to change though, he stayed home cooking and cleaning. He was trying hard to redeem himself but I didn't trust him as far as I could see him. A week later I got the call.

"I'm calling to offer you the position starting Monday." The office manager said.

I was smiling from ear to ear. It worked! I hung up the phone and screamed.

"Thank You Jesus!"

Jimmy hugged me and I hugged him back. I started working that Monday and I felt great. I felt important. Jimmy couldn't hold his money over my head anymore. I had my own and I had plenty of it. I loved my job and I especially loved my coworkers, especially Judy. We became best friends quick. She was funny and we had a lot in common so we could vent to each other. Some days she would come to work puffy eyed and sometimes I would, but we always cheered each other up. I loved my friend. She wasn't like my friends back home. She was educated owned a home and worked her whole life. Judy invited me and Jimmy out one day with her and her boyfriend. I was excited to be around different folks. Grown folks. We all met at her house and had drinks. I was instantly nervous because Jimmy was drinking Hennessey. He laughed and we actually was having a good time. The four of us proceeded to a club downtown and got a VIP booth. Me and Judy were laughing and enjoying the night. We walked to the bar and ordered a drink and a couple guys walked up to us. We both turned away and continued to order our drink. Jimmy came up behind me and asked why I was talking to those guys.

"I wasn't, chill out." I said.

"Bitch you all in niggas faces you disrespecting me." Jimmy grabbed my arm and walks me back to the VIP section yelling.

I didn't say anything, because anything I said was going to piss Jimmy off. I sat at the leather couch in our VIP section.

"Wasn't nobody talking to no niggas quit tripping." Judy said walking up fast behind us.

Jimmy didn't reply. Judy's boyfriend walked up and she told him what was going on. He was ready to leave, we all were. We walked outside to the car and Jimmy grabbed the back of my weave and pushed my head forward. I stumbled and swung my arm back at him. We got in the back seat of my coworkers car. I was so embarrassed. I felt like I was finally on the right path working and meeting new people. My life here was different than my life in my hometown. I erased that drama. The fear from the break-in, the girls everywhere I turned, knowing my man was sleeping with everyone. I was miserable there. I loved my new life but Jimmy had to bring it here. As soon as the car pulled off Jimmy back handed me in my mouth. I grabbed my leather Gucci bag and hit Jimmy in the face. Blood trickled down his mouth. Jimmy wiped his mouth.

"You better not fucking touch her. I'll shoot the shit out of you." Judy yelled.

I knew her man carried but I didn't know she did. If she was bluffing Jimmy believed her and that was all that mattered. Jimmy yelled and called me stupid bitches half the ride home. We came to a stop light and I got out the car. I couldn't take anymore. Judy jumped out behind me and told her boyfriend to go chill him out. We walked to her house which was closer than mine and Jimmy was there. He walked up to me and snatched my purse and got in our car and left. I didn't go home. I slept on Judy's couch in my heels and dress. I was so humiliated. I hated him so much. I had to get away from him. I need to stop talking about it and do it.

CHAPTER 8

I'll run so far
 Almost in hands length of stars
I don't care about the money
 Fancy things blinged out cars
Even when you're good
 The bad times too hard
Always thinking were so close
 Yet were so far
I can't keep trying
To heal scars
Always feeling
Like I'm looking through bars

Jimmy was passed out on the couch when I got home. I went to the kitchen and got garbage bags and went to our bedroom and started packing his clothes. Jimmy woke up from the noise and came in the room crying still drunk.

"I'm sorry baby I'm scared somebody going to take you away from me." He slurred.

I didn't say anything. I just kept packing his clothes.

"I ain't going nowhere. I'll kill you first" Jimmy declared as he snatched the bag out of my hand and pushed me on the bed.

"You better not have cheated on me last night, this my pussy."

I jumped off the bed and went in the kitchen too make some coffee. Jimmy came up behind and handed me a red Cartier box with a two and a half carat princess cut diamond ring with a one and a half carat band crusted in diamonds.

Aletta H.

"I'm sorry baby. I love you with all my heart. I know I'm fucked up but I just don't know how to love. I do know I can't be without you." Jimmy said getting down on his knees.

Tears flowed down my eyes because I believed him. He knew he had a problem but he loved me and I loved him. I just wanted Jimmy to be faithful and control his drinking and his tantrums. I wrapped my arms around him and we both cried.

The following weeks were going great. Jimmy spent most of his time at home or with me. We were in love and nothing was getting in the way of that. I saw the change in Jimmy and I continued to work and become better. We were a family. We had the grandkids over all the time, going on outings and having sleepovers. Jimmy and I were Granny and Papa. It was beautiful. I couldn't ask for more. Even when Jimmy drank he was happy, he was sweet and he would talk and be silly. I recorded him singing R Kelly songs and you can hear me laughing in the back ground. I forgave him, I always did. I gave him another chance and he finally was everything I want need in a man.

I'm going to be his wife
We put away the knifes
Bout to have a happy life
I let go of the past
Like my parents this will last
No more pain no more sad
No longer a child
Bout to walk down the aisle
My father would be proud
I'm kept
 His baby doll
I trust I have faith
Birthday,
 Death day
 Our wedding date

The next couple of weeks I looked for wedding dresses and started to make plans. We planned the wedding to be on our birthday the following year. My father passed on that day so we were just trying to make it special and marry on that same day. We had about ten months before our special day. I planned on wearing a powder pink chiffon dress with a mermaid fit, an eighteen inch Brazilian Remy weave layered with a part in the middle, a silver tiara and silver Tiffany necklace and bracelet set. I had already ordered my silver Louboutin's. Jimmy planned on wearing an all-white double-breasted suit with a powder pink tie, a white Dobb with a silver band and a powder pink small feather coming out. He had platinum accessories. We were about to stunt. I thought we were Jigga and Bey. We were about to shut it down. We planned to marry at the same church where my father's service was at. I had planned my bridesmaids in all white form fitting dresses with silver small veils pinned to an up do and powder pink strap around the waist with the same Louboutin's I'll have on.

Our plan was to go to Vegas for our honeymoon. Jimmy and I always wanted to go to Vegas together. He had been before but we wanted to go together. We were lucky at the casino together. We'd won $15,000 one year on our birthday. Most of our date nights were at the casino. Jimmy had plenty of cash and I had my own but used his when we gambled. One night we were drinking, planning the wedding and Jimmy wanted to go to the casino. We couldn't find any one to drive us. I don't play like that in the car, I wasn't riding with a drunk driver. Jimmy got mad and decided to go by himself.

I didn't object. I just knew I wasn't going. I was worried about Jimmy but I didn't want to fight. We were doing so good I was hoping he would change his mind, but he didn't and grabbed the keys off the table and left out the door. The casino was about forty minutes away, so I called when I thought he got there. He answered and said he was there and that he loved me and I wished him luck. I wished Jimmy luck and went to sleep.

I woke up the next morning and got ready for work. I was worried Jimmy was in jail or hurt so I called his phone and it went straight to voicemail. I continued to get dressed and went to work. I knew if I didn't hear from him by noon something was wrong. I also thought that if he didn't call me until noon and he alright, he stayed the night at the room and he called me when he checked out dropped off his monster. I wasn't trying to think like that but I was. I watched the clock as I checked patients in and out. Twelve o'clock came and it was time for lunch. I punched out and walked to my car. My phone rang, it was Jimmy.

"Hey baby what you doing I'm down the way I came here when I came from the casino." He stated

Down the way meant he was in our hometown. He was on some shady shit and I didn't have the strength to go through the pathetic motions.

"I will see you after work." I coldly replied and left it at that.

Aletta H.

Here we go again
Here we go again
This man not my lover
 He my enemy
We not even friends
It got to end
It got to end
Maybe I'm tripping
Maybe it's nothing at all
My intuition screaming
Don't fall
Don't fall

Maybe it's my fault. Maybe I should have just gone with him and chanced my life on the highway to the casino. I can't say for sure. I'm just going to be still and wait. What you do in the dark always comes to light. A couple of days go by and I get a call from my favorite aunt.

"Can you talk, is Jimmy around you?" I replied no, already knowing I'm about to hear something about Jimmy.

"Yes, I can talk." I say, bracing myself.

"Girl, I was getting my hair done and the whole time this chick bragging about this new dude she met from outta town. She said he got a girl, so they on the low. She also said he pays her for sex and took her to the casino the other night. She met him on a dating site."

That's was it! That was the confirmation I needed. There wasn't going to be a wedding but I was definitely keeping the ring, he forfeited it with his infidelity. I was done with him and it was nothing else to talk about. Life was going to get better for me by any means and I'd rather be alone than to walk around dumb and feeling inadequate all the time. My insecurities were growing. I felt unattractive. Felt like my sex wasn't shit. I just wanted the love I gave him in return. That faithful love that unconditional love flaws and all. Those flaws couldn't include being intimate with other girls.

Jimmy was putting both our lives at risk. I had people who needed me.

Jimmy got home later that day and his clothes were packed up outside the door. I went to the store earlier that day and changed all the locks.

I checked myself into a room a couple blocks down the street because I didn't even want to see his face or listen to him try to explain. Jimmy started calling my phone constantly and I turned it off. I pulled my Kindle out of my bag and started reading *Prayers That Bring Change* Kimberley Daniels. I used that book as a weapon against everything going on in my life and I always felt better when I was done reading it. I read that book all night reading over sections that I could feel in my soul when I was reading it repeating them over and over in my head. I eventually fell asleep and prepared myself for a fight.

Jimmy wasn't leaving me that easy. Out of all those girls he paid for sex I was with Jimmy when he hit rock bottom. I loved him the same. I used to say I was with him for financial stability but I was with him because I loved him with all my heart. I wanted so badly for him to love me the same. I couldn't pretend anymore. I was getting older and I was wasting time waiting for Jimmy to be right. I woke up the next morning and went to work. I was scared he would come to my job but he didn't. At lunch I went to my house to see if he took his things. He did he also kicked the door in and my apartment was trashed. All three of my sixty inch televisions were gone. Jimmy took most of my fancy clothes and my mink coat, the same one Kia wore in her Getting Sum Head video. I figured he would do something like that, I was prepared to get my comfy life swept from under my feet.

I went to the nearest Rent-A-Center and picked up a TV for my living room and made arraignments to pay it off in 90 days same as cash. I wasn't going to let that become an issue so I started fixing things on my own. I really didn't care about the clothes but he took my jewelry box that had earring in it I took out my father's ears when he passed. I was going to let that go too until I talked to him later that day.

"Hey Bae, I don't know what you tripping about but I'm done with the back and forth." Jimmy said when I finally answered the phone.

"Jimmy, can you please give me my father's earrings back. Everything else you can keep. You bought most of it so it was no big deal." I politely responded.

"I'll drop them off to your mother's house." He said calmly and we both hung up.

I was shocked he was letting go. Jimmy didn't love me. Everything was okay when I was quiet and he could do whatever he wanted, as soon as I stood up for myself he walked away. I laid in my bed and closed my eyes to meditate. I remembered while I was reading my prayer book, I chanted in my head, *Lord if he's not going to be right take him away.* I said it over and over again. Is this what I really wanted? To be alone? To struggle trying to take care of my family.

I knew it was the right thing to do and I was sick to my stomach thinking what values I installed in my children allowing all the abuse over the years. I started to walk blindly in faith. I knew God had me and that's all I needed. I was going to believe in myself. Shoot, I had a nice job and had just bought myself a car. I looked around and life didn't look so dim. I was beautiful inside and out. I heard a voice in my head say, *the meek shall inherit the earth*, and I believed it.

Jimmy called everyday drunk and frantic, cussing me out saying I would never be anything with all the kids. He called me fat, ugly and did everything in his power to break me. There was something inside that wouldn't let that happen. A week had passed and I was getting my bills in order and reading and writing poems. I was healing myself. I started getting calls from his family members and friends saying Jimmy was drinking heavily and that I needed to come get him. I ignored their wishes. Nobody came and got him when he was whooping on me or when he was at the strip club on stage licking stripper's pussies. I was good.

****

I was invited to a baby shower by a close friend. I was nervous, wondering if Jimmy would be there; he did business with her man. I went anyway because I had to get out the house start to reclaiming my life. Jimmy still had me scared to go outside and he wasn't even there. I stopped at Walmart to pick up a small gift basket. I didn't have much cash but I didn't want to show up empty-handed.

I parked on the street on the opposite side of my friend's house. There were people getting in and out of cars, so I didn't notice Jimmy's sister pull up with a car full of girls. She was a part of a motorcycle club and they always traveled deep. When she saw me, she pulled over her car in front of mine so I couldn't cross the street. I pretended I didn't see her and grabbed the bag out the back seat. When I turned back around, everybody was out of the car. Three more girls and a gay dude were standing blocking my path.

I never had a fight, so I tried slipping through the cars to get away. Jimmy's sister pulled out a can of mace and sprayed it in my face. My face burned like my skin was peeling off. I tried to get back in my car but she grabbed me by the back of the hair. Her friends started swing at my face and body while kicking me at the same time. I swing my arms uncontrollably at them and closed my eyes. Some guest from the baby shower noticed the commotion and came outside to see what was happening. I was still standing swinging so the group couldn't get me on the ground. Jimmy pulled up and just sat in his car watching. His friend started yelling at him to get his sister her friends, that it was and unfair fight.

Everyone that was with her finally backed up and I charge toward her. We both hit the ground with me on top. I balled my fist and beat her face as hard as I could until she screamed for help. Jimmy jumped out the car screaming for me to get off his sister. I got off her, picked up the mace can she had drop and ran toward Jimmy and sprayed him. Jimmy shook it off like I sprayed water on him and grabbed my arm.

I snatched away and charged Jimmy again and before I reached him Jimmy punched me in my stomach and I could hear air come out. Jimmy's friend tried to get between us and Jimmy pulled his gun on him. His friend ran back in the house while Jimmy stomped me to the ground and his sister digs to my face in. The crowd intervened and pulled me away.

I was exhausted. I was simply trying to get in the house and get some air. I wasn't leaving the house after that unless it was an emergency. I was ashamed. My face was scarred up like she used a razor blade on it and my eyes were burning. I was sick of people seeing me scarred up. I just wanted to get Jimmy out my life.

The next morning I opened up my Facebook and I was tagged in someone's status. I opened it up and it was a video of me getting beat up by Jimmy and his sister. I watched the video over and over again. There were over forty comments. Some of them said that's a shame but the ones that got to me were the ones were people were laughing and joking about the fight saying it looked like I got into a fight with Edward Scissor hands and lost.

CHAPTER 9

I had a dream that my dad and I were talking on the couch that changed me forever.

Daddy you're not gone
You didn't leave me alone
You're planted inside my soul
I can hear your voice daddy
Still telling me right from wrong
We talk in my dreams
Sometimes you pushing me on a swing
Still your little girl
Conquering this cold world
You always said I was chosen
I was a selected few
Through your love
I've always knew what to do
I heard my daddy's voice say
You got to take the good days with the bad
The bad days make you appreciate
The good days you had
Continue to do your best continue to grow
Forget that other stuff girl you can't help it if "fools don't know"

I needed to hear that, I need to remember how it felt. I had to do better. I had someone watching over me. I wasn't going to let him down. I got a call one night saying Jimmy was in the club flashing a gun drunk. Everyone felt the need to call me when Jimmy was acting a fool. I felt he was my out of control son. Most of the time I went to pick him up I would be praying he wouldn't be mad, but not this time, I wasn't going. Jimmy needed to grow up, enough was enough. A couple of his friends got Jimmy out before it got ugly. There were a lot of people who knew him and knew he got ignorant when he was drunk. The caller was a girl, she had a bad speech impediment. I couldn't understand what she was saying so I had to go in grandma mode and translate her infant speech.

"You need to come get Jimmy he been acting a pool out here without you girl." She mumbled.

"Jimmy is grown and he is doing that to himself." I replied and hung up the phone.

I was awaken by my phone ringing. It was three o'clock in the morning it was Jimmy. I was worried he was in jail so I answered.

"Hello, hello." I got no reply but I could hear talking.

This dumb nigga had pocket dialed me. I turned up my volume to hear what was in the back ground. I heard Jimmy's voice talking to someone.

"I'll give you whatever you and your kids need, anything. I'll get your kids anything just let me eat your pussy from time to time."

My heart dropped, I couldn't believe that I was hearing this with my own ears. I knew it was what he did but I never heard it with my own ears.

"My kids need everything babie." A female responded.

What the fuck? Was this that same retarded bitch that called me earlier to come get Jimmy? This bitch thought I was a joke, she was probably screwing him the whole time talking about her and Jimmy was just friends and she was dating his boy. I knew then that Jimmy would screw anything and anyone. Somebody was going to kill him about that. I yelled in the phone as loud as I could.

"Fuck you Jimmy! You stay with that illiterate bitch."

Aletta H.

I called and left texts all night. I was devastated; I couldn't believe this was happening. Jimmy didn't answer any of my calls. It didn't matter, nothing he could say would change things. That was it. The baby, the abuse and now this. My heart was broken. Deep down I was hoping Jimmy would change but this was proof that he wouldn't. I continued on with my life without Jimmy, worked and paid all my bills. I had a lot of damage to fix so I stayed to myself. I couldn't deal with another guy dogging me the way Jimmy did. I eventually talked to Jimmy on the phone, my weak heart needed to hear from him, but we weren't getting back together. Jimmy said he was going to make it up to me and we were going to be back together. I knew deep down that wasn't going to happen. I had come so far and I was ready to move on. I was going to stay strong but our frequent conversations felt like I was losing.

Everything for me was falling in place. I prayed the same words every night.

"If he's not for me, God take him away. Take him away."

A week later a mutual friend called me. G Dog said Jimmy was caught with his girlfriend in the middle of the night. She was driving his car and he was drunk shooting in the air. When the police pulled them over Jimmy had ten grams of heroin on him along with the gun. Jimmy led them on a high speed chase and jumped out the car to run. A police officer broke his arm during the take down so he was also charged with assault. He had prior felonies, so that was the end of the road for Jimmy.

I started balling. I couldn't believe he did this to himself, to us. I still believed inside we were getting back together and he would change. I didn't know how to live without instructions. I was lost.

Jimmy got ten years in federal prison, no good time. God had taken him away. I was left to continue. Jimmy called daily and turned into the man I always wanted over the phone. I was taught early on not to listen to men in jail. They will say anything to get mail and commissary. I listened to him and it made me feel better about the whole situation. He couldn't hurt me in there. Jimmy still ran most of my life from there he was in my head more than I knew. Sad as it sounds, I thought he protected me, while all the while, he was the main abuser. I left my children's father and after the jail incident, he didn't come around at all he didn't want the responsibility of being a father. He only pretended to love them when we were together pretending we was a family. I really felt like Jimmy was my family. He was like a father to me but with abuse.

I only had a couple friends in the new town. I was scared I was going to fail but I continued. I started writing blogs on top of working ten hours a day at the doctor's office. I just wanted to be normal. I talked to Jimmy on the phone daily for this first six months, then it went from an occasional letter here and there. I had started to heal. I wanted to forget the drama I had been through with Jimmy and God took him out my life for good.

I missed Jimmy. I was in love with the abuse, it was all I knew. The big picture for me wasn't so bad. I had an apartment, a new car and a great job but it always felt like I was on the edge.

My blogs started to get recognized. In most of my spare time I was writing poetry and blogs online. I found this urban poetry site and joined. To my surprise I was the featured new artist several times. I started to believe in my writing. That part of me I was sure about. Nothing or nobody could take that from me. I started to interact with other poets. I checked my inbox and there were a message from the owner of the poetry site I wrote for.

I am very impressed by your work. I would like to sit down with you and discuss some avenues for you to take to get our work published.

I agreed to meet with him for lunch the following day. As soon as he walked in the restaurant I was intimidated. His name was Bashee. He was six feet five inches tall with dark cocoa skin. His body looked chiseled to perfection under his white button up shirt and khaki pants. He wore small frame glasses and he had perfect white teeth. I had never interacted with a grown man of such. All the guys I dealt with were thugs or drug dealers. They were all street. Bashee walked up and extended his arm to shake my hand. I could barely look him in his face. I thought he could see the shame on my face. I didn't feel confident enough to be sitting at the same table with him.

He sat down and pulled some papers out his briefcase. Bashee smiled at me almost like he was flirting. I'm sure it was just in my messed up mind. Bashee compared my poems to Maya Angelo, my writing to Terry McMillian, Iyanla Vanzant. I didn't believe what he was saying, I had started to get the feeling he was going to try to sell me something. Bashee paused and took a deep breath.

"I've been fascinated by you ever since you joined my poetry group. Your words flow from your wounds in perfect harmony. Not only that but I'm fascinated by your beauty, your strength. If it's not too much to ask I would like to spend time with you. I would like to write with you." He professed.

I was shocked, I couldn't believe he was interested in me. Most of the poems I wrote were sad. Poems about my heart being broken and damaged. I looked up forcing myself to give Bashee eye contact. I smiled and thanked him for talking so highly of my work. I grabbed the napkin off the table and wrote my number on it. I didn't think he would call but he did the next day.

Writing has always been a hobby of mine. I never knew it would catch the eye of others. I never thought guys looked at me as beautiful or strong. Bashee was from my hometown. I thought he knew everything I went through and felt sorry for me. I didn't want a shoulder to cry on. I was scared this was just another man trying to get laid, another rollercoaster ride that I would place myself on. I was terrified of dating, especially Bashee. My insecurities would ruin it.

CHAPTER 10

Prior theft
Carefully watching my steps
Taking slow breaths
Picking up what's left
Scared of next
Trying to be at my best
With a hole in my chest
Death of my love
Come to rest
Always a space between
Emotionally unclean
EVERYTHING is
Recollection of a bad dream
I get so close
Refilling the holes
And slip back away
Till my heart stone cold
I protect what's left
From the prior theft
I got a lot of it back
But valuables were kept
Nobody is welcome
No matter where they come from
Involvement with me
Is the beat of my drum?
I'm paused in this state from the valuables that were kept
I protect
 What's left?
 From the prior theft

I spent a lot of time on the phone with Bashee. We talked about his writing and stuff he did with the community in our hometown. He would mentor low income children in our hometown without fathers. Bashee shared with me that he used to sell drugs and gang bang but changed his life from a seven year prison sentence. He found the Nation and was Muslim and it changed his way of thinking about the world. Bashee had scars from past relationships and loss also. We would talk all through the night. Some days Bashee would text me the start of a poem and we would go back and forth battling. I enjoyed Bashee. He was my friend. I enjoyed the attention and time he spent with me. Bashee treated me like the woman I always knew I was. He treated me like a queen. Bashee was gentle with me. He didn't force me to agree if I disagreed. He listen to my ideas. Bashee always ask me to read my poems aloud, knowing I was shy. I would not hesitate to try, voice shaking and all. Eventually I was reading aloud to my family and friends. When I smiled it was genuine not forced.

I was happy. I was happier than I'd ever been and I felt confident. I continued to write my blogs and began writing an outline for a book. There was so much bottled inside I knew that I could help others going through the same thing. I still had a long way to go. I was getting my anxiety disorder under control. I never had to be medicated. I just had to overcome my paranoia. I didn't trust anyone, anything and I was scared to open that door again. I was falling fast for Bashee. I gave all my love to the wrong guys all the time, but now I got a handsome gentlemen wanting to be more and I was scared to death.

I figured if I let him in and trusted in him, it would hurt worse in the end. I fantasized about Bashee all the time.

I started working on my physical appearance. I wanted to be comfortable in my skin. I had let myself go. I started working out and eating better. I made sure I wore light makeup to enhance my full lips and big eyes. In no time I transformed, thirty six, thirty, forty. I was like a Coke bottle. Bashee would give me compliments and his smile made me feel like melting. I wanted Bashee too but I didn't want to ruin the friendship we shared.

Jimmy would call and try to tear me down every chance he could. I stayed in contact with him because he was still like family to me. I felt sorry for him though. I did computer visits and Jimmy had me walk the computer around the house so he could see if anyone was there. Jimmy still talked about marriage and about us getting back together. I knew by the time Jimmy got out I would be far gone from his grasp. I was trying to support him. I still loved Jimmy but I knew that we could never be together again. As much as he hurt me I wasn't equipped to hurt him.

Bashee and I were getting closer as the days went on. Every morning I would get a "*good morning beautiful* text and every night *good night beautiful*. Life was going in the right direction for me although I still endured abuse from Jimmy over the phones and letters. It was easier to shake it off knowing we didn't have to be face to face. I relocated to a smaller apartment when Jimmy got locked up. I had acquired a lot of stuff so it was nice, just not what I got accustomed too. I was a regular at the spa getting $150 lash extensions and $95 facials.

I got so used to having my hair done every month in $450 weaves. I was like an angry child, mad cause I had to pay my own bills. I had to go back to basics, cooking meals instead ordering out. I had to humble myself. I had to learn how to be grateful for what I had, grateful for a new start. I made sure I was capable of paying my own bills. I was living check to check though. I didn't want to fall in the trap needing financial support from anyone. My apartment wasn't as nice as my prior apartment but I was comfortable. It was mine.

Bashee and I worked on getting a publisher and started to submit manuscripts. I didn't think that I would get found. Bashee was more experienced than I was as far as writing. I continued submitting chapters as I was writing my first book. All I could think of was finishing the completed project. Bashee and I spent countless hours discussing it. I appreciated his expertise and pushed myself to get through it. On one of our long days at the library Bashee walked me to my car. He stood there looking in my eyes and placed his hands on my face.

"I'm not going to hurt you." He whispered and placed his lips ever so softly on mine.

It felt like time was standing still as our lips touched. I wrapped my arms around Bashee's chiseled body and embraced him. I got in my car and drove home. I was up all night thinking about Bashee. My guards were at attention and I was ready to cut him out my life, scared of being hurt again. Scared that all the repairing I had done with myself would fall back apart. I prayed for guidance. Inside I knew I wanted to be with Bashee but I wasn't allowing myself to let go of the past. It was hard with Jimmy calling and taunting me.

I couldn't turn my back on Jimmy, not now. I couldn't leave him in the position he was in. I knew I would never have a healthy relationship as long as I stayed connected with Jimmy. I wrote my last letter to Jimmy I needed closure.

Dear Jimmy,

I pray for you every night. I hope this time goes by fast and you come out a better person. I've allowed you to place so much anger and pain inside me and I want to get better also. I love you and I'll never forget you. It's time for both of us to let go. I am no longer your piece of property to do as you please. I forgive you. Please forgive me for not standing up for myself, allowing you to think it was ok to treat me that way. It wasn't. I can't keep allowing your calls and letters putting me down. I can't let you control me anymore. All I ever wanted from you was your love. I only said I was using you for money to make myself feel better. I wanted to live happily ever after with you knowing that nothing about being married to you would be happy. I'm trying my best to love me again and maybe someone else one day. So I'm ending our communication. I'll send you money every month to buy commissary. You took care of me and my children financially and I'll do the same for you. I'm taking my heart back. My dignity. There's something I want you to think about Jimmy. I always thought you would change, you would get better. You accepted me as I was, a weak scared little girl who didn't stand up for herself. You wanted to marry me in that condition. You should want better for yourself also.

Goodbye

Reminisce

And Jimmy replied.

Bitch I always knew you wasn't shit. I took care of your broke ass with all them bad ass kids. It don't matter if I don't get out in 20 years hoe, you going to always be my bitch. You can fuck with a nigga if you want to, both y'all bitches can get killed. You always talking about me cheating on you, but that's dumb shit. As far as my putting my hands on you, you was starting the shit with your fucked up ass. I'm going to act like I didn't get that letter from you. That was some stupid shit going through your scary, weak mind. You need to be thanking me for saving your rat ass. You wouldn't be shit without me remember that and just because I'm here ain't changed nothing. So you better answer the phone when I call. I can send somebody for you.

I knew it wouldn't be that easy. Jimmy always had one over me. Jimmy knew I was scary. He knew if he was out I wouldn't be saying none of that and my life would be the same. I would be miserable. Miserable with a bunch of material stuff. I ignored his calls and continued working. I consolidated my bills and started to work on repairing my credit. Slowly my credit score came up but not enough to buy a house. It really looked like I had it together. I was barely paying my bills. Borrowing from Peter to pay Paul. Taking out payday loans to fill in the blanks. I was struggling, but from the outside it looked all good. I had a fancy car, a nicely furnished apartment and a decent paying job. I knew I had a purpose.

I focused harder on my writing. I started to believe in myself. It became a performance when I wrote poetry. The words fell from my mind. My story became a mental movie that I was creating.

In the meantime, I was growing closer to Bashee. I started to trust Bashee but I still didn't want to be more than friends. We both were physically attracted to each other. Our mental connection overrode the physical. He was my avenue to express myself vocally and I loved that about him. I daydreamed about him and I being together but it always ended up being a nightmare. I knew loving him would be new territory that I hadn't experienced before. I didn't think I was equipped for that, not yet. We continued our friendship and I was intimate with him only in my dreams.

I imagine your embrace
How you look at my face
I imagine how your lips taste
In my dreams I give you my all
Frequent visions of you catching me
While I fall
Unaware manifesting,
My destiny,
My blessing to be
Dreams become reality
With feelings so deep
Changing life occurrences
While you sleep.
Trapped in a box
Everything ain't always as it seems
Spiritually free
Emotionally clean
But only in my dreams

I started to get responses from the submissions of my work. I didn't know a lot about it. I knew I shouldn't have to pay a fee to get signed to a company. I turned down a bunch of companies I heard nothing about. I got an email one day from a well-established company offering me a contract. I couldn't believe it. They believed in my sample enough for me to join their team, a best-selling team. I was happy and nervous at the same time. I held the contract in my email for a week. I spoke with Bashee about it. He felt I should have signed it as soon as I got it. It wasn't about the monetary value at all. It was the accomplishment.

I felt I would fail. I started to flood my own mind with negative thoughts of failing. I started to sabotage myself before I even tried. I prayed and asked for guidance and strength. I was still damaged, I just handled it differently. I embraced it and allowed it to make me a better person. There was still a lot of work to do with me despite that. I signed the contract and continued working on my book. I started interacting with the group I belonged to and would watch as their books hit the top 5 in the urban category. It pushed me. I wanted to see my book finished. Every free chance I got I wrote. I scribbled ideas and poems on loose pieces of papers that were floating around in my purse. I carried around a flash drive so I could open up my book at work and work on it during my breaks. I was determined to get it finished I stayed up for days at a time only taking breaks for food and naps. I had a feeling it would change my life. I felt inside that this was my purpose, to share myself.

I finally finished my book and I submitted it to my publishers. I was nervous but confident at the same time. It took around two weeks after the publishers got it for it to be finished. I was shaking when I pushed the submit button. There was no turning back from there. I called Bashee later that night and sent him my manuscript. I talked to him about the anxiety I felt, how I was overwhelmed with feelings of failure. Bashee reassured me and told me it was my time. Bashee filled my mind with positive thoughts of accomplishment. I heard a knock on the door and it was Bashee. He was talking to me while driving to my home. He had already bought a bottle of Moet and two pink champagne glasses. Bashee had roses and chocolates. I was surprised he would do all that. I opened the door and he grabbed me close to his body and kissed me passionately on my lips. I was tense, I didn't know how to react but my lips kissed him back.

Bashee sat on my red leather sofa and motioned for me to sit by him. I sat next to him and he put his arm around me and whispered in my ear.

"I'm so proud of you."

A tear rolled down my check and I buried my face in his chest. His smell permeated my senses and I began kissing him. We were both enjoying each other that night, I felt triumphant. I finished my book. I was breaking down the concrete walls I had surrounding my heart and opening up to Bashee. We fell asleep on my couch wrapped around each other's body fully clothed.

Over the next week I was a nervous wreck waiting for my publisher's response. What if they don't like it?

What if they cancel my contact? I read my book over and over replaying the scenes in my mind.

I connected my email to my cellphone anxious, to get there mail. Until one day I got an email from them.

We have received your manuscript and we love it! We have passed it to corporate. We feel you could collaborate with some of our top writers. This will be a top seller and we are so happy to be working with you. Your book will be released in the upcoming weeks. Watch your email for the completed book. Also try to clear your calendar for the next couple of months as you will have a full schedule of events and book signings to attend. You will go far in this business!

Congratulations

I couldn't believe it, I was shaking. I was an author. I made it. Over the next few weeks everything was moving fast. My book was released on my birthday and it hit number one for three weeks in a row. I started my second book immediately because I didn't want my readers left in limbo. Bashee was acting as my manager. I would send him emails and correspondence while I was at work and he would make calls and respond to everything on my behalf. I continued working at the doctor's office because it was still all so unreal. I was scared it would come crashing down. My security was at my nine to five there and I wouldn't let that go. I wasn't scheduled for my first royalty check for three months, *so* I still needed to survive.

After a month of my book maintaining sitting at the top of the charts, my life went in a whole different direction.

Aletta H.

I knew there was no turning back when I got invited to do a special on the Oprah Winfrey Show that paid me fifty thousand dollars. I took on writing full time and hired Bashee as my personal assistant/manager. I had never been on a plane and was now on one every two days. I had a glam squad that followed me around and an unlimited black credit card. I didn't think about what was going on, I was just working. I was confident enough to speak on television and promote my book. I became a brand. I was speaking at events on television and was now a household name. I became an instant success over night.

After about two months on the road with Bashee. I came home to pack my stuff and moved into a five bedroom ranch by the lake with an in ground pool, surrounded by fifteen acres of privacy. I checked my mail and it was a letter from Jimmy. I opened the envelope before I could even think not too.

I promised I'd kill you first. You and Bashee.

I balled the letter up and threw it away. Bashee was moving in with me I couldn't imagine not having him by my side through all of this and we were obviously more than friends at this point and everybody knew it. Later that night Bashee and I was going to get some take out. We had the movers coming the next morning, it was our last night at that small apartment. We pulled back up and noticed a small car parked across the street with the lights on. We continued to walk in the house until we heard someone call his name. We both turned around and before I knew it Bashee pushed me on the ground and pulled a gun out his pants and I heard fireworks. Two guys got out the car with guns and start shooting back. I run to the front door and up to my apartment.

"That's Jimmy's bitch you hoe ass nigga! Watch your back." A guy yells as tires screech off.

Bashee came in the house with blood all over his chest and collapsed on the floor. I called the ambulance and the police. Bashee was in bad shape and I was to blame. I sat by Bashee while the nurses came in and out. Bashee had been brought back after dying twice. The doctors weren't sure if he was going to be fully functional. I just wanted him to wake up. He lay there lifeless because of me. I couldn't handle it. I promised myself if Bashee woke up I was going to love him completely.

I would go up to the hospital with my laptop and write. I would talk to Bashee's lifeless body for hours. After two month at the hospital Bashee fully recovered. He had no memory of what had happened and I was scared to tell him it was because of me. I loved Bashee and I promised myself to love him and I was. I had to be honest with him, so I told him what happened later on. Bashee just had a blank stare. He didn't blame me. Bashee wanted to protect me from Jimmy.

We moved in to our new home. Bashee and I were busy from all the new found fame so we erased that incident. Bashee continued to work with the youth in our hometown also. We started a charity organization for underprivileged youth and started opening help centers for the community. A year after my first book release Bashee and I planned a trip to the Bahamas. We both needed a break since we were working nonstop. I made sure I filled Jimmy's account every month since Bashee got shot.

I was scared of him and I felt I could pay him off. I still got letter and I changed my number so many times I stop trying.

Jimmy would always get it. I never opened the letters. I was scared of what they would say. I just wanted to erase him but Jimmy kept resurfacing. I woke up the next morning of our trip ready to go we drove up to board our plane and parked in valet. Bashee and I went in the airport and my phone started to ring, it was Jimmy. Bashee answered the phone and told Jimmy to never call my phone again, it was over it was done and hung up. I turned off the phone and put it in my purse. I could tell Bashee was getting fed up with my stalker Jimmy. I just prayed it wouldn't run him off. We arrived to our hotel, which was a hut that sat on the beach surrounded by similar huts. Two exotic women approached us with hula skirts on and handed us a drink served in a coconut shell. We walked in our hotel and the room and it was covered in pink roses. A lady in a soft pink long dress was there playing a flute softly. There was also two guys in black tuxedos and white gloves. One of the men approached me with champagne and the other with a tray of chocolate and strawberries. I was dumbfounded as to why they were there. Bashee grabbed my hand and motioned me to the bed. The flutist started to move as she got further in her solo. One of the gentlemen handed Bashee a small silver bag. He got down on one knee.

"I love you more than I love me, I promise I won't hurt you. Please be my wife." He sweetly asked as he pulled out a platinum four carat diamond solitaire ring. It looked fake. He was still kneeling and I could see it sparkling. Bashee grabbed my hand and kissed it. He placed the ring on my finger.

I looked at Bashee and his face was wet with tears and he was shaking.

"Yes." I managed a breathless response as I nodded my head.

We spent the next few days in the Bahamas completely over taken by the scenery and each other. We returned back happy to announce our engagement.

I gave my all in my relationship with Bashee. We were in love. He was my business partner and everything was wonderful. I trusted Bashee. I let my guard down completely. I was ready to love and to be loved. Bashee had just gotten out a long term relationship when we first became friends. He spoke of their relationship and how she cheated on him, how he felt he could never truly be loved. Bashee shared some of the same inadequacies. I was happy to have been given the chance to love him. I wasn't letting my insecurities or fears ruin what we had. I wasn't letting Jimmy scare me from a happy life.

****

We got an offer to film our wedding and broadcast it. I was nervous but I agreed. I wanted my fans to always have access to me. The filming started a week before the wedding. There were cameras set up all over the house. I had a cameraman following me in the back seat of my car everywhere we went. I was overwhelmed. I had to keep my composure in front of the camera which started to get difficult.

Bashee would leave to get a break from the cameras leaving me to plan most of the wedding on my own. Bashee felt like it was all about me and he didn't want to be involved in the taping so he would do occasional appearances with me having dinner or a breakfast scene. It felt like we were growing apart. His explanation was he needed to be alone. He got tired of the cameras taping his every move. I was worried about our relationship. I didn't want Bashee to feel like he was riding my bus. He was a big part of me growing into a brand. I start contemplating getting a pre-nup especially with his change in attitude.

I was going to surprise Bashee and showed up at his office across town. I had a cameraman follow me. I just planned to have a picnic lunch in his office. I wasn't there to discuss the problems we started to have. I walked in to his office and was dryly greeted by his receptionist. She was an older lady he met mentoring kids. She was married to his cousin. She stood up before I reached his door and said Bashee was in a meeting, she would let him know I was there. I took a seat. I had an overwhelming feeling to walk through the door. I heard a soft giggle come from his office and I busted through the door. Bashee was sitting at his desk. There was a slim white women behind his desk straddling him with her dress pulled up. I rushed over to them and grabbed the white girl's hair and slung her on the floor. Bashee tried grabbing me as I had a fit in his office knocking things over and swinging my fist at him. The white girl ran out the office. I noticed all this was being filmed. I tried grabbing the camera and the cameraman took off. Bashee stood there as I came apart crying. His receptionist came in and tried to calm me down.

Bashee grabbed his coat and stepped over my body as I laid there hysterical.

I went home and threw out his stuff. I grabbed a bottle of Don Julio and drank the night away crying. I was awaken by my phone ringing and saw that it was my sister I hadn't talked to anyone about it so I was surprised when she asked if I was ok. I was silent. She said there was a clip on all the news channels and online of the prior day's incident. My heart dropped. I hung up the phone and walked to the front door. The whole yard was full of media. I couldn't face the world. I caught Bashee cheating and now it was being aired on national television.

From the moment I hung up with my sister my phone rang nonstop. I went to my room and packed a bag. I called my brother to come get me and drop me off at the airport. I was going to spend some time with my publishers and get a room and concentrate on work. I wanted all this to go away. I wanted to get in front of a computer and type this pain away. This new numbness. My mind was screaming I told you so and my heart had opened a new wound. I wanted Bashee to make it all better. He started calling my phone but I didn't answer. I knew I would forgive him sacrificing my own heart. I thought if I took him back he would feel it was ok and continue cheating.

My brother pulled up and Bashee got out of the car with him. I was pissed! Why would my brother bring him here and he just humiliated me on national television. I ran to the door cameras flashing following my brother and Bashee to the door. I wanted to cuss him out but I was humiliated enough. I was going to let him have it when he got in the house.

As they walked in the house my brother's face was balled in a tense position.

"You better fix this shit Bashee. You got my sister out here like this." My brother said as he grabbed Bashee by the shirt and pushed him towards me.

"Baby I'm so sorry, she means nothing to me. You were getting to busy for me and I thought you would leave me." Bashee said turning to me appearing to be ashamed. "I feel like I just work for you now."

I didn't even let Bashee finished talking as I slapped him across his face.

"It's over Bashee. I don't want to be your wife. You are no longer my assistant/manager. I'm walking away. You promised you would never hurt me and you did." I said heartbroken.

I didn't want to talk any more, I just needed to get away. I got in the car with them and we left to drop Bashee off to his old apartment. My brother drover me to the airport and sat with me and waited for the plane.

"You're too good for that sis, your chosen remember. That nigga was lucky you wasted your time with him. You've always been special in my eyes sis. You're famous, you don't need no man to validate you.

It was in God's plan with or without Bashee that you would make it. He just lucked up at the right time that's all." My brother said trying to encourage me and lift my spirits.

Bashee was just enjoying the free ride. Maybe my brother was right. I tried to take his advice but Bashee loved me before the book deal. I never thought he was using me he sacrificed his career for mine. I wiped my eyes and thought about his words. I was thinking about relocating closer to work but I was unsure. I didn't want to be so far away from my family so I was just taking a break. I came back seven days later.

CHAPTER 11

Be still child
Hand your burdens to me
Don't let nothing alter you mentally
Don't allow a wound to form
Go above
Be more
A test of endurance
Challenging your growth
Already been here
Already been wrote
On a pedestal
With a crown
Listen close while
The trumpet sounds
Follow you around
Hear my words
As I lift you while you down
All the stuff you been through
All you have seen
Manifesting your reality
Into Your destiny
It's more than a dream
You know your worth
You're a queen

Dangerously In Love: Blame it on the Streets

I ignored Bashee's repeated attempts to contact me and beg for my forgiveness. I focused on a new series of books, a survival guide series for young's mother. The books would be to build self-esteem called *Queens*. I gave Bashee full control of our charities so I wouldn't have to see him. I even gave Bashee a chunk of money because deep down, I thought he helped me to grow in that person I was becoming. I still wanted to know that Bashee would be okay financially.

I couldn't believe it when Bashee started doing interviews about us splitting up. He was on every blog spilling the beans about my secrets. Bashee told the press about my ex Jimmy in jail harassing him and the shooting. Bashee was making money off of cheating on me. It made it easier to forget him until, the mail man was knocking on my door with a certified letter. I signed for the letter and went back into my house. It was from an attorney. I opened it up and Bashee was suing me for $2 million dollars for agent and booking fees. I couldn't believe that bastard. I paid him good plus Bashee had access to all my money all the time. I called my attorney to let him know what was going on. I wasn't giving him a dime he actually owed me money. I was furious. I was hurt. How could he do this? I really thought he loved me and I still loved him.

I was prepared when court day came. There were cameras everywhere but I wasn't nervous at all. As the judge asked his attorney to introduce his case, Bashee jumped up from his seat.

"I don't want to do this, I want you back. I love you and I'm lost without you. I'm sorry!" He blurted out.

The judge started banging his gavel for order in the court and Bashee began walking over and stood in front of me. Bashee got on both knees and started begging me to take him back. I pull him off the court room floor, grab his hand and walked out. The media was yelling questions at us as we walked hand in hand to my driver and got in the car. While in the car Bashee talked the whole ride home about how he felt like he was going crazy without me. He said he almost finished a book of poetry me being the main character. He had my wedding ring I threw in his office on his pinkie finger and slid it on my finger. I'd forgiven everybody else, so I felt I had to give him a second chance. It hurt worse not to have him in my life.

It was scary taking him back but I did. I loved him. He still was the best man I had ever had. I was giving him a second chance. We started calling up and getting our wedding plans back in order. I opted out on a second taping of my wedding. It was going to be more intimate then I planned before. We were signing a pre-nup, especially with that court stunt he pulled. I wasn't taking any chances. I was shopping with my sister one day looking for shoes for my wedding. We were having a great day. It felt good to be able to financially take the burdens off my family and I did. We walked in a shoe store and started to look around for shoes for bride's maids. I went to the back of the store to look for Bashee and my son some shoes when suddenly a guy bumps into me, hard. I turned to look with my face turned up at him and it was Cle.

"Jimmy said answer the phone and write him." He snarled.

I almost fainted. I could smell alcohol on his breath and his nails were black around the tips. He wasn't that same casual guy I met before. Cle looked like the streets were kicking his butt and he was broke. I tried not to think it but Cle looked like an addict. His smooth skin now had small visible holes everywhere. His hair was in an afro matted to the back of his head. Rumor was when Jimmy got locked up he was snitching and by him and Cle being so close it cut him out the game too. My sister was still in the front of the store. I squeezed past Cle and rushed to the front with my sister. I grabbed her arm and pulled her up and ran out the store.

I had forgotten about Jimmy. Jimmy had been locked up for 4 years now and I thought he would have moved on by now. After he had Bashee shot I contacted the warden and had him issue a no contact order but I couldn't prove he had anything to do with it. Jimmy stopped contacting after that so I was surprised Cle said that. I called Bashee and told him what had happened and I drove my sister to her house and went home. I was paranoid. I felt like I was being followed but I wasn't. I got home and Bashee was waiting on the porch for me when I pulled up. I was trying to act unaffected by my earlier conversation with Cle but my body was shaking. Bashee put his arms around to calm me. I needed to move out of the state to feel safe from Jimmy. I didn't speak on it but I had vivid nightmares of him beating me, feeling overpowered, helpless. Jimmy was a demon that I created. A demon that I stored inside of me name fear. The thought of him sent chills down my spine.

Bashee agreed about moving out of state after the wedding. We needed to hire new people to run our charities and to take over Bashee's mentoring program. Jimmy still had awhile to go, and I was determined to out of his reach by the time he was released.

In our state its mandatory you get tested so your partner is informed of your statuses before marriage. Bashee and I both had a doctor's appointment. I wasn't worried my prior job carried good insurance and I was up to date on my exams. Bashee had been tested for STDS when we first became intimate. We both got tested. Bashee wasn't up to par with his yearly exams. He ate healthy and exercised all the time and he appeared healthy, but he always complained of headaches. We both thought he needed new glasses or it was due to spending long hours in front of the computer. We waited in the waiting room for our clearance papers. The lab was on site so everything was done in a day. A nurse came out and called Bashee's name. We both stood up and the nurse said she needed to talk to him alone. I sat back down and she handed me my clearance form. Bashee walked back with the nurse. Time stood still as I thought of what could be wrong with Bashee. Bashee walked out with the same clearance paper I had and a white folder. He shook the doctor's hand and we walked out the door.

By the time we reached the car I was asking what they said. Bashee put his seat belt on and handed me the white folder.

"Beating cancer, treatment options for beginning stages". Bashee said.

He said they told him his blood counts were off. They further tested it and detected brain cancer. The whole drive home me and Bashee were silent. We knew we couldn't leave, we needed to be close to our family our home. Bashee called the next morning and made an appointment with an oncologist. Everything was depending on Bashee's his health, our wedding, moving. I would do anything for Bashee. Bashee went to the appointment to get further test run. The test came back showing he had spots of cancerous cells in the frontal area of his brain. The doctors informed him he caught it early but still needed chemo treatment to kill the existing cells. We only had three months until our wedding. We postponed it after we got back together to avoid the paparazzi.

The doctor informed him what was included in the treatment. He would be sick, weak, maybe some memory loss. Bashee knew he had to do it so he set his appointment for the next day. I waited in the waiting room while he got his first treatment. Bashee walked out normal and we went home. Later that night he woke up vomiting and having diarrhea at the same time. His temperature was at one hundred and two when we decided to take him to the ER. They hooked an IV to Bashee and gave him morphine to help him relax in pain. I stayed the night with him in the hospital. By the morning he was feeling a little better and they released him. Bashee had five treatments to do. Being injected with a chemical to kill everything in his body, even the good things just to build himself back up and go through it again. I felt bad for my love. He was sick and I didn't know what I would do without him. I stopped writing and focused on Bashee.

I hired nurses also to hook up IV bags to hydrate him and keep him stable after his treatments.

After the fifth treatment Bashee got retested and there weren't any traces of any cancer cells but the doctor couldn't say for sure if they were going to come back. He had to be monitored regularly. We continued on with our wedding plans, we had two weeks left. Everything was falling back in place. I had India Arie agree to sing as I walked down the aisle. The day before our wedding everything was still going great. I checked into a hotel that I shared with my mother and sister. I grabbed my purse to get my credit card and my mail fell out my purse to the floor. I had put it in there earlier while I was leaving the house. A letter dropped out from Jimmy. My heart dropped as I picked the letter off the hotel lobby floor. I put it back fast before anyone could see it. I went in the bathroom when I got into our suite and read it.

I just wanted you to know I haven't forgot how you played me and ignored my calls and letters. I got the money you was sending but that wasn't enough you should have been there for me emotionally. I got my appeal and my sentenced was lowered I'll be out next month I'm tethering at my mother's house. You can't hide from me anymore. And you tell that Bashee bitch ass I'm coming to get what's mine. See you soon.

My heart dropped. I couldn't believe he was getting out next month. I was terrified for me and Bashee. I continued to get ready for the next day. My wedding day I had thoughts of Jimmy fresh in my mind. I didn't want to tell Bashee until after the ceremony. I didn't want to ruin our big day. That morning came and my suite was packed with people, hairdressers, people running in and out with dresses and accessories.

I sat in the chair to get my hair curled. I was scared. My anxiety was setting in and I was nervous. The room got loud and I was scared something bad was going to happen, my past was resurfacing. I walked in the bathroom and put water on my face.

"Calm down. Calm down." I repeated to myself.

I imagined Bashee standing waiting for me as I walked down the aisle and the negative thoughts subsided. Jimmy made sure I lived in fear. I finished getting dressed and ready and then walked to the back of the hotel where a horse and carriage awaited me. I was dressed in an all-white taffeta gown with pink rhinestones around the waste. I had on a platinum tiara accented in crusted diamonds. I walked up to the carriage and my brother was already there. He was walking me down the aisle. My brother grabbed my arm and helped me in the carriage. We sat there waiting for our queue to ride in front of the hotel and enter. I thought about of my life and got choked remembering how far I had come. I thought of all the abuse I endured by the hands of my baby daddy and Jimmy. I felt so sorry for that girl taking all those blows. The only thing holding me on to that past life was Jimmy and I was going to get rid of him somehow.

The doors were opened when we pulled up to the front. The bridal party was going in paired up. I got out of the carriage and my brother walked me down the aisle. India Arie was playing a piano in the front singing *Ready for Love*. I got to the alter and Bashee grabbed my hands.

He stood there with a neatly trimmed face and beard. He had on a cocaine white suit and tie. He had on white gators and a white Dobb. Bashee looked like a king standing there. I loved him and I was ready to live the rest of my life with him. The ceremony was over after we recited our poetic vows to each other and everybody moved to the room next door for the reception. It was the happiest day of my life. I was married. I danced with Bashee all night. I don't think Bashee knew that was the first time I danced in public. Bashee laughed as I moved my rhythm less body to the music. I laughed too because I was feeling the music and let myself go.

Over the following weeks I worked with Bashee on a screen play and continued with my other projects. I never mentioned the letter I got to Bashee and Jimmy getting released next week. I wanted to erase it. I added extra security to our home and gated the whole property. I knew I had to tell Bashee what was going on so, I sent a text message about the letter from Jimmy and explained that I was scared to tell him. Bashee didn't reply. Later that night when Bashee came home he slammed the door. I walked up to him and tried to hug him and he snatched away.

"Why would you wait so long to tell me about Jimmy? Were you planning to go back to him? Why did you have to think about it first? What, are you waiting for me to die? You like niggas beating on you? We are married. I own you." He spewed.

Those last words stood out. I couldn't believe my ears.

"You don't own me, you're tripping." I said as calmly as I could.

Bashee walked up to my face and nodded his head, there was fire in his eyes. Bashee walked up stairs to our room and slammed the door. I didn't know had gotten into Bashee. He had always been so gentle with me. I knew I was wrong for not telling him but I didn't want to ruin our big day. I walked up the stairs and walked in the room. Bashee was lying on the bed with a towel over his head in the dark. I walked over to the bed and sat by Bashee.

"I'm sorry baby. I've been having headaches and I'm worried the cancer is coming back." Bashee said softly. "I've been forgetting things and having rapid mood swings. Seems like I'm edgy all the time. I just can't get a grip on things. I'm scared baby, I'm sorry for yelling at you. I don't want to die. I don't want to leave you here alone knowing that nutcase is still stalking you."

I laid on Bashee's chest and rubbed his head till he fell asleep. Bashee was in no shape to go against Jimmy if confronted. I had to protect Bashee from him. Bashee was hesitant about going back to the doctor but after his headache didn't go away he had no choice. Bashee was right, the cancer had come back and he was put back on chemotherapy immediately. Jimmy was to be released the prior day, but I didn't hear anything from him. Bashee's first treatment was the start of something bad. He went downhill from there.

Bashee could barely walk. His veins shrunk so the doctors put a port in his chest they could get to quickly instead of searching for his shallow veins I had to call the ambulance because he passed out in the bathroom and stop breathing. I prayed Bashee would get better but it seemed as time passed it got worst. I took care of Bashee from morning to night. I put my work off till he got better. Bashee lost weight and became frail. He was unrecognizable. I was scared I was losing Bashee and prayed over him every night.

While Bashee was fighting for his life Jimmy started reaching out to my family members saying he just wanted to see me. They didn't give him my number or tell him where I lived they knew Jimmy was bad news and they felt threatened by him contacting them. I went to the police station to get a restraining order against Jimmy and I couldn't provide proof so it was denied. I hired security to watch my home. I was terrified and didn't go anywhere unless I had to. Jimmy was going to kill me and I could feel it. Bashee on the other hand wasn't in good shape. The doctors said his cancer was spreading rapidly and Banshee's mental state was slipping. I hired a full staff to help with his care. Bashee would forget who I was some days or where he was. Bashee's temper was getting out of control. He would throw food across the room at the staff. He would have tantrums and have to be sedated. Bashee got to a point where he couldn't dress himself or even use the bathroom on his own. He was angry he was sick and losing his mind at the same time.

I went to the back of the house where I usually wrote to take a break from everything going on. I cried for Bashee I didn't think he was going to make it.

I laid in my chair and my cell phone rang it was Jimmy.

"Hey baby I'm not going to hurt you, I just want to see you. I know I did you wrong and your married to that sick nigga now but I just want to be friends. I've changed I know I threatened you but I had nothing to do with Bashee getting shot. I'm trying to be nice but if I don't see you soon it's going to get ugly so quit playing with me and come see me."

I hung up the phone and checked on Bashee. He was lying there still. Something wasn't right he was too still. I called for the nurse and she came in and checked his vitals. They were faint Bashee was slipping away. We were newlyweds and I was watching my husband die. The nurse called the ambulance and pumped breaths in his body till they arrived. Bashee was rushed to critical care. The doctor informed us he had suffered multiple strokes. They were having a hard time keeping him stable but they were still working on him. They would know by the morning his status if he makes it through the night. I called my sisters and mother. I cried so hard in the lobby of the hospital staff had to come out and assist me. Every time the door opened up I would jump up thinking its news about Bashee. I stayed up all night pacing, praying aloud. I was pleading with God not to take Bashee from me. I couldn't endure any more loss. I felt like I was cursed.

Morning came around and my sisters left to get breakfast, I stayed in the lobby. The doctor came out and sat next to me.

Aletta H.

"I'm sorry ma'am Bashee is hooked up to life support the cancer has spread to most of his main organs and it's just a matter of time until the machine will be doing all the work. He is officially brain dead." He said compassionately.

"Nooooo! Lord please no, don't take him away from me. Why are you doing this to me God? Why do you put me through so much? I can't take this. I don't want to do this." I screamed, tears burning my face.

As I was screaming my sisters rushed back through the door and wrapped me in a huddle. I was trembling. I stayed with Bashee lying there hooked to those familiar machines that I had seen many times prior. That same beeping sound imbedded in my head from my nephews death. I wanted to have hope that he would get better but he wasn't. The doctors were waiting for me to take him off life support. I had just gotten married earlier this year now it was ending with a funeral. I kissed Bashee on the lips and signed the papers and walked out the room.

Bashee had twin teenage daughters that spent a lot of time with us. They were upset with Bashee for leaving there mother not knowing the circumstances that led to the break up. She cheated on him with his brother and he caught them following her one day at a park having sex in the bushes. Bashee and his brother weren't close after that so I wasn't surprised he didn't show up at the hospital. Bashee felt his brother was always jealous of him because his brother was an ex crack head and was still treated as one in the streets.

That made it even harder to know the woman he loved his whole life was cheating on him with his crack head brother. I walked out and his daughters were coming in with their mother. I stopped them before they got to the door and they put their arms around me. I told them that they took him off life support and he died instantly. I explained that he was brain dead and the machine was breathing for him. I vowed to Bashee that I would care for them, especially now that there mother seemed to also be addicted to crack.

I didn't want to go home so I took his daughters and we checked into a hotel suite until the next day. They were somewhat shy with me but they opened up about there's mothers drug abuse and different men. They wanted to tell Bashee that they forgave him for leaving and they understood why he did. They had a year left of high school, they were smart like their father. I told them I would send them to any college they wanted. Their faces were similar to Bashee's. It felt good to be around them. One of the twins even had his laugh which brought tears to my eyes every time she giggled. Bashee always tried to get custody but the courts wouldn't allow it because of the felony on his record that was 16 years old. I sat down and let them make all the decisions for the service what he was to wear and what songs were to be sung. They both wanted to recite one of his poems but later declined. They stayed with me until the day of the funeral but had to return to finish the school year off.

My sisters took the notes we made for his service and took care of everything. They made sure I had little to do with it as possible. I didn't have the strength to write a poem for his obituary. I was just a shell.

Aletta H.

I was going through the motions, once again guest of honor at a funeral. I didn't have access to any valium this time and I wasn't going to take them again since I almost got hooked. I knew I had to ride this out to the end with my eyes open. I was torn to pieces, zoned out, staring off into nowhere. I was a widow and I hadn't even been married a year. My sisters planned a small service at our hometown church. The service was short and sweet. I had Tamela Mann sing *Take me to the King* in a cappella at his service. That's always the hardest part at a funeral the sad songs confirming your gone. I wanted to go see the king also.

I had thoughts running through my mind of suicide. I had start planning in my mind who would get what. I thought about how I'd do it. I was at a low point and I didn't think I could live anymore without Bashee. I was unrecognizable as I sat there with a black veil over my face the whole time. My family would come up to hug me and try to lift it of my face and I would move away before they could. Underneath that veil was a broken woman. I looked like I was dead. My eyes were black and swollen. My nose was red and peeling from constantly blowing it. My lips were dry and cracked from dehydration. To make matters worse, I could barely speak my voice was raspy. My head hurt so bad from the light I didn't want to live. There was a black cloud over me, I was cursed.

The family all came to my house afterwards. Bashee's twin teen daughters sat on the back steps holding each other. Everywhere I turn there were pictures of the wedding, our honeymoon, and the many trips we took together. Bashee's hospital bed was still in our room piled with boxes of medicines and supplies.

My sisters stayed with me until they felt it was safe for me to stay alone. I sat in the back of the house lying in my chair. My office had papers everywhere and I hadn't written anything in some time now. I had the world in my hands only to lose it in the blink of an eye. I could still smell Bashee as I walked through the house. Everything was like a nightmare I couldn't wake up from. I cried for hours every night like a baby balled in fetal position for their mother. I stopped bathing and combing my hair. I could barely eat.

My sister had her pastor come pray with me daily and I began to get better. It was a slow process but I got better. I couldn't write anymore because it brought back too many memories of how we met. I had royalty checks coming in from the books I'd already written, so I was still very well off financially. I knew I had to write though, it was therapy to me. The fears set in so deep I felt that more bad news was always coming. I would jump at noises. My hands were constantly shaking. Every time I closed my eyes I saw Bashee. I called my publishers for help. I had two books left on my current contract and I couldn't even turn on my laptop. We were like family at that point. We made tons of cash and I was speaking to them daily. I didn't answer my phone lately and they had been trying to contact me. I spoke with them and thought it would be a good idea I got away for a while. I was hesitant. I looked like I was terminally ill. I had to snap out of the funk I was in and continue to do something I didn't want to with Bashee not here.

I had thoughts of Jimmy often. I thought he was just waiting for the dust to settle and come after me. I was at a point in life that I didn't care if he did I was tired of running, tired of living in fear always thinking he was behind me. I packed my bags and went to settle in out of state where my publishers were located. They met me at the airport and I checked into a nearby hotel. I brought my laptop because I was going to try my hardest to get back to writing. I felt the loss of Bashee and everything I had been through. I had to write a book about it. I had to close everything up on paper. I settled in to the hotel and took a shower and put on some pajamas although it was still daylight, I wasn't going sightseeing. I didn't need to fight off the media while they try to take pictures of me in such a vulnerable state. I ordered some food and wine up to my room and opened my laptop. I sat there staring at the screen, I didn't know where to start. I decided to try a poem to see what came. I knew it was going to be about pain and loss but I didn't know I would cry all the way through it.

CHAPTER 12

Defeated torn apart to shreds
Closet in my life are dead
I walk under a dark cloud
Following me
Even when I'm in a crowd
I have to start over again
Everything positive comes to an end
How can you pick yourself up?
When you can't stand
How can you fight?
With no use of your hands
How can you pray?
When you prayers are unanswered
How did I lose my husband to cancer?
I hear my daddies' voice
Baby girl you're not a quitter
Trying to be still
I'm close
Almost bitter

By the time I realized I wrote that poem I was on the second chapter. I was spending every second I had writing away the pain. I talked with my family and publishers daily but I spent most of time in that hotel room. I stayed there for two weeks and I had finished my book my autobiography but would get it published as fiction. I wanted to get back in the spotlight. I needed some attention even if it was just the attention of my fans. I needed it. I agreed to do some appearances. I was called to do the Ellen show and talk about my book. I had to sit there and pretend I was talking about a fictious character and I knew it was me. As I spoke of her I would choke up. It caught the attention of the audience how passionate I was about my book and it went to number one right away.

I returned home to a place I dreaded to stay for a couple weeks as I was in the process of transitioning to a new home I'd recently purchase closer to my publisher. When I arrived at my house my brother was pulling off. He had been staying there while I was gone. I thought Jimmy would catch word I was gone and break in and wait for me. My brother greeted me with a hug and kisses and grabbed my bags and walked me in. The whole time he was talking about my newest book. Trying his hardest not to bring up Jimmy or Bashee. Finally on his way out the door he gave me another hug.

"I'm here for you sis. Stop worrying about Jimmy, I'm going to get that crazy ass nigga. I promise you." He assured me.

It was a relief to know that he was concerned but I knew nobody could stop Jimmy if he was coming for me. My children who were all grown now, had decided to move in to my house when I relocated so they were in and out bringing their clothes. It felt good to be around them. I had been so busy. I didn't see them much I would just send them money. I took care of my whole family financially. My oldest daughter walked in my room as I was packing Bashee's clothes to give to the charity we had in our hometown. She sat on my bed.

"Is everything alright?" I asked her.

She smiled faintly and looked away. I panicked.

"What's going on, you're not sick are you? Please don't say you're sick."

"No mom." She replied. "I just though I needed to tell you something before you hear it from somebody else."

I sat there quiet bracing myself. I couldn't take any worse news I would have a heart attack. She said for a long time she knew she wasn't attracted to men. She said after watching all the beating I took and heartache from an early age, she knew she didn't want to indulge in a relationship with a man. I was still silent in awe. I knew where this conversation was going.

"I was scared to talk to you about it. I didn't know how you would feel. I didn't want to embarrass you or add to your problems so I kept it to myself. I've been dating a girl for almost two years now and we are getting married." She revealed.

I didn't know what to say. My oldest daughter was a diva. She was a girly girl. Never in a million years would I think I would be hearing these words coming out of her mouth. I didn't know what to say.

"I'm going to love you no matter who you love as long as they treat you good." I finally said to her.

I gave her a hug and apologized for putting her through so much as a child. I didn't mean for them to have seen so much. I tried to make up for it all with money, and now I had plenty of it, I realized money couldn't take away what they had endured. Money didn't take it away for me either, it was almost worst. I just found an outlet for my pain.

"Have you read my latest book?" I asked her.

"I'm sorry Mom, I didn't. Do you have a copy?" She said with a guilty expression.

I opened my bag and gave her a book. She went in the room next to mine. I could hear her on the phone telling her girlfriend she told me and everything was okay. She told her she wanted her to come to dinner so everyone could meet her. I was uncomfortable because it was new to me, not because I thought she was gross. I wasn't against it, it was just something I had to get used to. I planned a big get together two days before I was to leave. I called family from all over to see me off. I didn't hire caterers I wanted to get back to my roots so me and my mother stayed up all night cleaning and seasoning meat. We made potato salad, baked macaroni and cheese, greens, black eyed peas, cornbread, and baked beans. We cut up fruit and vegetables and made platters. My sister baked several cakes and pies. It was nice being all together cooking, it reminded me of my grandmother's house.

As we set up for the gathering, I was forcing negative thoughts out of my mind. I kept thinking Jimmy heard about it and he was going to show up. People start arriving and I felt safer, he couldn't kill us all. Midway through the get together, my cousin Belgium and his wife showed up. He had an envelope in his hand. He walked to the front of everybody and opened it. He asked for everybody to be quite and proceeded to read. It was addressed to me.

This letter is to inform you that you have been nominated for writer of the year. Others in your category are, David Weaver, Sapphire, Iyanla Vanzant and Terry McMillian.

Aletta H.

I ran up to my cousin and snatched the letter from his hand. I couldn't believe I was in a category with such top authors. Belgium's wife opened up her bag and pulled out a bottle of Ace of Spades and popped the top. Everyone started to applaud and a rush of sadness came over me. I wanted Bashee there. He was a big reason I came as far as an author. He believed in me so I believed in me too. I didn't think the pain was ever going to go away, everything reminded me of him. Every happy moment from this moment on was accompanied by sad. I didn't think I would ever meet anyone like him again. I vowed to never date again.

My daughter walked up with a beautiful mixed girl with long brown hair and eyes. She was tall like she played basketball or modeled. She introduced her as her fiancé. I stood in front of everyone to get their attention, pulling my daughter and her soon to be wife up. I introduced her as my new daughter in law and congratulated them on the engagement. There were stares coming from the crowd you could tell some of them didn't agree. I didn't care I just wanted my daughter to know I accepted her and her fiancé no matter what anyone said. My sister (the Christian) pulled me to the side and started preaching about being gay is a sin; that my daughter is going to hell if she continues. She said I need to make her start coming to church with her. I ignored her and continued drinking.

Everyone was drinking and getting turned up. It was wonderful. I was surrounded by people who loved me and who were proud of me. People who knew my story and accepted me as I was. As the night grew and people started to leave, Belgium noticed a car parked in the front.

Belgium and my brother walked to the front of the house guns in hand and before they got to it, car it sped off. Not fast enough to notice Jimmy sitting in the passenger seat. They jumped in my brothers Range Rover and went after him. I was nervous something was going to happen to them. They were both drunk and Jimmy was a killer. He wasn't scared to die and had nothing to lose. They came back several minutes later and said they lost him.

Belgium and my brother stayed at my house that night. It was the last night I was going to be there. I hated having to have protection around me. I would give any amount of money for Jimmy to just leave me alone. I went in my room and grabbed my phone. I strolled through the numbers looking for the number Jimmy frequently call me from. I try several number until I reach him.

"Listen you bum bitch you better leave me the fuck alone before I kill you myself! I'm not going to be hiding because your weak ass can't let go." I shouted.

"Bitch you out here balling. You sent me that bullshit while I was locked up but you ain't have nothing for me when I got out." He shot back.

I knew it Jimmy was broke he needed some cash. When he got out early his business partners cut him off, they thought he was snitching. Jimmy's street credit was obsolete and nobody trusted him.

"How much do you need to leave me alone Jimmy?" I asked completely fed up with the entire situation. "How much do you fucking want to leave me alone and to buy a new bitch Jimmy?"

"Half a million." He said laughing.

"What? I don't have that! I ain't doing it like that." I spat.

I lied I had over seven million dollars in the bank. I was just trying to talk him down.

"Yes you do bitch. I looked up your net worth on Google. Don't play with me." Jimmy sneered.

Knowing Jimmy was doing research on me snapped me back. I knew how Jimmy was and without money, he had homicidal tendencies. Money was his security blanket. Jimmy could buy his status back in the street.

"Ok, ok, I'll give you the money. I'll have my brother drop it off to you in the morning before I leave." I relented.

"Oh yeah, I forgot you was leaving tomorrow that's a bad house you just bought. I've seen it. I was there the last time you were you didn't even see me, ha!" He teased.

"You lucky your dirty ass spent most of the time in that room. I had it all planned. I stayed many nights next to your rental car, you know the white Benz you was driving. Girl, I'm everywhere." He continued to taunt me.

Chills ran down my spine as I thought of him following me. I always felt like he was but I just thought it was my paranoia.

"I don't want your brother to bring the money I want you too I want to see you one last time. Shit! You don't think I need closure too? I love you so much. I know you rich now and you better than me. It's just hard to let you go baby." He spoke.

His words rang in my ear as I imagined my zillions getting ripped from my scalp. By any means I was getting this over with. I had to meet him. I had to do this on my own or he would torture me forever. I agreed to meet with him at the library. I chose there because it was two buildings away from the sheriff's station. I wasn't taking any chances and I was carrying a gun. I knew Jimmy and he had a quick temper. I was just going to listen to what he had to say, give him the money and he would be gone forever.

The next morning I woke up early so I could go to the bank and sign all the necessary paperwork to take out that amount of cash. I carried a pink and white Hello Kitty book bag that belonged to my granddaughter.

I didn't want to look like no drug dealer with a briefcase full of money in the library. I circled the library several times in my car. I just wanted to see him pull up. Moments later Jimmy pulled up and he has a morbidly obese monster in the car. I pretended I didn't see her and walk in the library. Jimmy jumped out the car and followed me in.

"Damn baby you look nice. You can tell you got a couple dollars. I wish you quit acting stupid and give a nigga another chance." He said.

"I would die before I got back with you, Jimmy. Bashee opened my eyes to a different love and it was the total opposite of what you were offering." I snapped.

I continued into the library and checked in at a computer station. Jimmy checked in to the computer next to me. I handed him the bag, he unzipped it and smiled.

"There you go Jimmy I wish you the best now will you please let me live my life." I said almost pleading.

Jimmy's head was still focused on the bag. I got up and started to walk to my car and Jimmy followed me laughing. I put my hand on my waist which housed a 22 and opened up my car door. Jimmy kicked my door shut and my gun fell. I tried picking it up and he kicked it under the car and slapped me.

"I told you bitch this isn't a game. You always going to be my bitch!" He yelled.

I tried to yell and Jimmy punched me in the face and knocked me out. I woke up several minutes later and Jimmy was driving my car and the monster was in the front. My hands were tied behind my back and I was gagged with an old shirt that smelled like sweat and funk. I couldn't believe it was going to be that simple. It was a set up. I knew not to trust Jimmy. I did this to myself. I started kicking at the door and trying to scream. Jimmy drove to an alley and jumped out. He opened the back door and had my 22 in his hand. Jimmy put the gun to my head.

"Game time over. We're about to spend some time together like I said." Jimmy said.

The monster girl was in the front with her arms crossed.

"I thought we were just picking up some money from her. I knew you still wanted her. Get me the fuck out this car, I'm done with you Jimmy." The monster shouted.

Jimmy walked to the front of the car, opened the driver's door and shot her in the head. Jimmy walked around to her door and opened it and pulled her out on the ground in the alley. I couldn't move.

I could only watch. My eyes wouldn't blink I was so terrified. I knew Jimmy had been a killer but I'd never seen him do it. Jimmy jumped back in the car.

"Bitches need to learn to shut their mouth. Fuck her and that baby probably ain't mine anyway." He chuckled, clearly deranged.

I had to think of something quick or I wasn't getting out alive. I balled in a fetal position in the back seat and wept. Jimmy drove for about two hours I knew we were far from my home but I didn't know where we were at. My family probably thought I was on the plane headed to my new home but I was far from there. Jimmy pulled up to what looked like an old gas station and yanked me out the car. He untied my mouth and opened his mouth and sucked my lips in his.

"Please Jimmy, I gave you the money please don't do this. I won't tell. I'll give you more money. Please Jimmy……..*I love you.*"

Jimmy turned away and stood there for a second then turned back around and hit me in the head with the gun.

"You don't love me, you don't know what love is. You used me then threw me away like my parents did. Don't nobody love me." He snarled.

My body collapsed to the ground. Jimmy drug me into the abandoned gas station. I was barely conscious. I had given up. I couldn't fight him. I felt this coming. I knew he was going to kill me one day. I thought of my father, nephew and Bashee. I was going with them and it didn't feel half bad. I surrendered. Jimmy won.

Jimmy laid my body on a pile of wood chips. I was going in and out of consciousness. I could feel him tear of my shirt and pants. Then I felt his hands in my panties. I was praying to pass all the way out. Jimmy flipped me over and pulled down his pants. He got behind me and shoved himself inside of my ass. It felt like he was fucking me with a knife. I could feel blood running down my legs. Jimmy put his hands around my throat and banged my head on the ground. I passed out. Several hours later I woke up still on the pile of woodchips. Everything hurt and I was pig tied and couldn't move for some relief. Jimmy sat across from me, eyes blood shot red with a bottle of Hennessey in his hands.

"I'm sorry baby. Why did you leave me? I thought you were the only person on this earth that truly loved me and you showed me you was like everybody else. I can't take knowing that you don't love me anymore, I can't take it." He sobbed.

I looked in Jimmy's eyes and almost felt sorry for him. I had to use his vulnerability. I scooted over to Jimmy and put my head on his lap. Jimmy took the gag from my mouth and kissed me. I kissed him back I was fighting for my life. Jimmy untied the rope and I stood up.

"I'm sorry Jimmy I never meant to hurt you. I didn't think you really loved me. You cheated on me and beat me for saying something. That's not love Jimmy that wasn't fair." I spoke softly.

Jimmy put his hands over his face and started to sob harder. "I don't know what's wrong with me. I'm just fucked up. I just wanted someone to love me. I needed to know I was special enough for somebody to love me."

"I did love you Jimmy, I did. I still loved you, eve after you beat me. That last letter I wrote you. The end when I said you should want more for yourself. I was talking about me. You shouldn't want someone on your arm so weak. Someone who will allow anything in her life as long as her bills were paid. You should've wanted better than that. I felt like I wasn't worthy of you. I was lonely when I got with Bashee. I didn't love him like I loved you." I continued.

I knew I love Bashee more than I had ever loved Jimmy but now was not the time to reveal that or let that get in the way of my safety. Jimmy pulled me in his lap like I was his child. I embraced Jimmy back thinking of the body he left in the alley, his baby mama.

"Jimmy you just shot your baby mother in the face. You don't love yourself; you have to learn to love yourself. Now what Jimmy? Back to prison? Take that money and run.

Just go Jimmy. I won't tell I just want to be left alone. I've been through so much and I just want to leave." I said.

Jimmy jumped up and pig tied me and gagged my mouth again. Jimmy grabbed the gun and walked out the door. I could hear the car pull off. I know he was not leaving me here to die. I had to get loose and get out of here. I didn't know where I was at. My head hurts so bad I could barely open my eyes. My private parts feel like they had been ripped open. I rocked my body back and forth till I get on my knees. I crawled over to the door. I couldn't turn the knob so I turn around and tried to lift myself enough to grab the knob and open the door.

I was finally able to get the door open and I crawled outside. There were no cars driving by and no houses around. I knew I couldn't crawl miles back to the mainland. I saw an old ax leaning again the building and I scoot my body over there. I place my bonded wrists over it and gently start cutting the rope off my hand. It came off and I untied my legs and took out the gag. I was stuck in the middle of nowhere and I knew Jimmy was going to come back to finish me off. I ran straight to a wooded area and followed the road ducking so Jimmy couldn't see me if he pulled up. It seem like I was walking forever. I finally heard traffic coming and waited till I saw a steady stream of cars. I jumped in the middle of the street almost getting hit by a semi-truck. The truck pulled up and I passed out.

Several days later I woke up in the hospital. My room was packed with people. There were flowers covering every inch of my room. My mother was stroking my hand when I woke up and she kissed my face. My whole body was trembling. My mother motioned for me not to talk and said I need to be careful. I was threatening another seizure I had to stay calm. Apparently while I was passed out I had back to back grand mal seizures. My body was stuck on the edge to have another one. I didn't say a word. I closed my eyes and I saw Jimmy's face. I jumped up and opened them and the nurses where rushing in to sedate me.

After I was relaxed my mother asked the nurses to give her some paper and a pen so I could communicate safely. I grabbed the paper and pen and wrote.

Get me away from here.

My mother stroked my hair and looked away. I grabbed the paper again.

Jimmy is going to kill me get me away from here, help!

My mother sat back next to me in the bed and began to speak.

"You can leave after court. There was a body found in the alley and Jimmy told the police you did it and said you were mad she was pregnant by him, you met up with him to try to rekindle your relationship and that's why he snapped and assaulted you." She explained.

"The officer also told us that they had you on surveillance withdrawing a large amount of money out of your account and that the bullet that killed Jimmy's baby mama came from a gun registered in your name."

I started breathing heavily. I could feel the tremble increase. Calm down, calm down, I thought to myself as trembling turned into involuntary jerks. The nurse rushed to me and inserted a needle in my IV bag and I could feel the trembling subside as it flowed through my vein. My mother said I had to meet with the police as soon as I was better. It took a few weeks in the hospital for me to well enough to go home. I was put on Wellbutrin for my anxiety and phenobarbital to control the seizures. I had my lawyer meet me at the police station to give a statement. When we got to the secluded room. The officer asked to me turn around and cuffed me. The officer informed me I was being charged with first degree murder and fleeing the scene of a murder. I knew I was innocent. I knew my fate wasn't behind bars. As the officer escorted me to a cell there was news reporter and the media in the lobby snapping pictures while I walked by. I dropped my head and kept it there not knowing if I was going to ever face the world again. Anger started to build up after I had to sit in that small cell waiting to get processed and out on bond.

That place

God took me to this place that smells of shame
Voices crying, plain guilt, pointing of blame
Bright lights, loud chaos, I can't escape my pain.
God placed me in front of my self alone
A place where my mind has nowhere to roam.
A place unfamiliar, a Place unlike home.
God took me to this place to recondition, reassure.
Concrete walls, Unclean floors as I stand spiritually pure
As I was alone I felt god by my side.
Unsettled emotions trapped inside
As I released and surrender my all.
Those concrete walls begin to fall....as I stood and
walked out the door.
God took me out of there but I left so much more

After securing my release with a million dollars and both home titles I was free. Jimmy had already been processed and got out on a fifty thousand dollar bond that he paid himself. He was charged with aggravated assault and tampering with a witness. Jimmy's charges were lowered because he gave that bullshit ass statement and was going to testify against me. I was fighting back. Jimmy wasn't going to get away with this. All that weak nice person I was is out the door. It was time for me to fight life back.

CHAPTER 13

Alter ego
I introduce you to me
My alter ego
Cold piece
Former street
Wounds deep
Mind on the grind
Never sleep
Quick to speak
Never weak
My eyes dry
From lie
Goodbyes
Asking God whys
My heart so cold
From my stolen soul
A love that was bold
Beauty and the beast
Both are me
Dollars signs
Revenge
Is all I see
I'm a product of the game
I'll never be the same
That level of pain

Aletta H.

The streets to blame
Cold piece will seduce you
Break your heart
Play you like a game
Stuck on start
She clearly here to stay
No more games
Cold piece don't play

Even when I'm done with this court bullshit I ain't going nowhere. Fuck that! Ain't nobody running me away again, nobody or nothing and I mean that. If I could take all that bullshit I'd been through, I could go through anything. Fuck that weak shit. Things were about to change for me. I went home that day and ran a hot bath. I soaked for about an hour contemplating my next move. I was tired of being the victim. I wasn't going to be old and bitter. I called my attorney over so discuss some ideas. He came by I was in grimy mode. I asked him could we pay the judge to drop my charges. He looked at me shocked. He knew how I'd handled almost getting sued by Bashee, so he didn't expect to hear that from me. I was done playing fair. I had the attorney tape my statement about the events from that day.

"I got a call the night before from Jimmy. He stated if I didn't meet him with the cash he was sending someone to kill my mother. I believed him since he had gotten my husband shot from prison, so I wasn't taking any chances. I went to the bank and got the money. I met him at the library where he and a girl pulled up.

We walked in the library I gave Jimmy the money and he snatched the gun from the back of my waist band Jimmy walked me to his car by gunpoint and I sat in the back seat. Jimmy rode a few blocks. Jimmy and the girl tied me up she was upset he didn't get more money and they started arguing while I sat tied up in the car. Jimmy shot her in the head. We pulled off and went to an abandoned gas station where Jimmy raped me in and out of consciousness pistol whipping me with my gun."

My lawyer turned off the recorder.

"How the fuck do I end up in the hospital half dead accused of murder? You need to fix this shit. I ain't even going to worry about it. If I go to prison for some stuff I didn't do, I'm coming for you." I warned.

My lawyer grabbed his briefcase and walked out the door. I grabbed my purse and my brand new .25 and went to the nearest liquor store. I grabbed a bottle of Don Julio and some pineapple juice. I got two packs of blunt sticks and texted my brother to find me some weed. I was self-destructing. I was hoping I would see Jimmy. I was blasting him in pure daylight. I'm not holding him up. He had to go. Fuck my career, fuck my life, fuck everything. As I was pulling up to my house my brother was pulling up I noticed he had someone with him and I walked in the house and let the door slam. My brother walked in and I turned around and Tony was standing there.

"Hey Ms. Famous I was in town and saw your brother and jumped in the car to see if you were alright." He greeted me.

"Yeah I'm good." I dryly reply.

Tony gave me a what the fuck look and I grab the weed from my brother and start breaking it down on my white marble table. My brother sat beside me.

"Chill out sis, I know this is a lot. Fuck Jimmy, we know you didn't do that."

I lit the blunt and take a big pull and pass it to Tony. My head starts spinning instantly and my eyes swell shut. I open up my bottle of Don and make me a drink. Tony came over to me smiling.

"So you gangsta now?" He laughed.

"Nigga I've always been gangsta, it's in my blood." I snapped. "I don't give a fuck with nobody says. I'm done being nice. I'm done letting motherfuckers do me anyway. I'm going off on everybody."

My brother passed me the blunt and I held it and smoked the rest. I filled my glass back up without a chaser this time and killed it in one drink. My brother and Tony stayed till they fell asleep on the couch. I think they thought I was breaking down but I wasn't. I knew how I felt and there wasn't any turning back. I went in the back room and opened up my laptop and begin making a timeline of the events that occurred with Jimmy how I begged for protection only to get denied. I dug up every letter he wrote and phone numbers he had called me from I was preparing my own case. I wasn't putting my life in that lawyers hand.

I woke up the next morning and my brother and Tony was still asleep on the couch. My doorbell rang and I went to see who it was on my camera system. It was my second eldest with her four children. I rushed to the door and hugged my grandchildren. My daughter walked in and I could tell she had been crying. I took the kids in the kitchen and fed them cereal and sliced strawberries. I sat by my daughter and she burst in tears. I then notice a small scratch above her lip and bruises on her arm.

Aletta H.

"I know your baby daddy ain't put his hands on you." I calmly said.

Her head was still down crying and I ran to wake up my brother and Tony. They jumped out of their sleep and I told them my daughter had been abused. My brother ran to his car and got a briefcase and brought in the back in the house. He opened it and started assembling a military type weapon. My daughter jumped and screamed.
"It's not his fault. I should have shut up. I know those girls don't mean anything he loves me and I need to just be quiet." She made excused for him.

I rushed over to my daughter and wrapped my arms around her. This was my fault they were living the same life I lived. They learned from me like I learned from my mother that it was ok to allow abuse, mental and physical. I never thought he would do that to her. His family was well known in our community and owned several churches. He was raised in church.

"Mom you know how I get sometimes. I'm frustrated and take it out on him. It's hard raising these kids I appreciate your money mom but I need help in other areas also. This isn't the first time he has hit me but this time I was scared he wouldn't stop.
I told him I was coming to drop the kids off to you so we could talk." She continued making excuses.

Before the last words came out her mouth there was a knock at the door. I looked through the camera and it was my grandchildren's father. I snatched the door open and put my .25 in his mouth.

"Come in woman beater. Punk you think this a game?" I yelled.

He put his hands in the air and walked in and I shut the door. My brother jumped up and sucker punched him to the floor. My grandkids start screaming witnessing the whole thing. I pull my brother back and point for their dad to sit down. My daughter sat next to him and grabbed his hand. I was furious. My grandchildren's dad covered his face.

"I didn't mean to hurt her. We fight all the time but when I saw our daughter watching me I realized I was teaching her it was okay." He began to cry.

I called his mother over and we discussed him getting some help or I would kill him. She told a story about getting a black eye picking him up from preschool as soon as she pulled up by his father. It was almost normal watching abuse as a child. I knew things needed to change and I was going to start some counseling programs for abused women and their children. The cycle had to stop. I wasn't comfortable letting my daughter stay at home until he was well in his counseling, so she moved in with me. Having my grandchildren around put a calm in me nothing could compare too. They slept with me and followed me around like I was god.

****

The trial was to start soon. My lawyer said I had nothing to worry about with Jimmy's record and the proof of his harassment and behavior was enough to bury him under the jail this time. I was back in the spot light.

The media was begging me to talk about the case but I didn't. I wasn't giving him the satisfaction of five minutes of fame. I would over talk them to spread awareness about abuse. After so many failed attempts they stop asking.

I walked in the courtroom and it was packed with people. I noticed a small frame lady similar in the face to the girl in the car with Jimmy crying in the back. Jimmy sat next to the prosecutor with a smirk on his face all dressed in a suit and tie. The hearing began and the prosecutor tried to paint a horrific picture of me committing the senseless murder. Then he called Jimmy up to speak. After stating his name, the attorney asked him to tell him about the events that happened that day.

"I've been in a relationship with Reminisce for almost ten years. When I went to prison we stayed in contact and she sent me money monthly. She told me she married her former husband for publicity." He lied.

His attorney handed the judge Jimmy's books from prison showing my monthly deposits. Jimmy was trying to play the victim. He said he was having a boy by the girl he shot and I was jealous, he said he loved her. The small lady in the back of the court got on the stand. She stated Jimmy was nice and he took care of them. That he had met her daughter while he was in prison and was going to marry her. I was looking horrible in the jury's eyes. I was looking horrible to myself. My attorney asked for a recess and we went to a room to talk.

"It's not looking too good for you. I know we have a lot of evidence but you sending him money meeting with him doesn't seem like you were that scared of him." He told me once we were alone.

I walked out the room and back in the court. After I gave my testimony and proof the court was adjourned. We were to reconcile the following day. The following day came and I was preparing to spend the rest of my life in prison. I walked in the courtroom and I heard a voice call out to me.

"Hey, hey!"

It was Tia the heroin addict he used to pay for sex who had his child. I gave her a dirty look and continued to walk to my seat. She stood up and sat in the seat behind me. Jimmy was looking over at her with hate in his eyes. She tapped my attorney shoulder and asked to speak to him in private. They came back only after a few minutes and my attorney had a sinister look on his face. He asked to approach the bench and he had new evidence. Jimmy's lawyer jumped up. Both lawyers and the judge went in his chambers court was going to continue after lunch. I didn't leave the room during the recess. I was jumping out of my skin when they returned. My lawyer motioned me out the court room back in the small room and was all smiles.

"Apparently Jimmy pocket dialed Tia the day of the events and she recorded what seem to be you and Jimmy's voices after the shooting." He told me. "The conversation included him saying he didn't care about her and the baby."

We got back to the court room and Jimmy had his head on the desk. I'm sure he knew now about the pocket dial also. Jimmy's lawyer rushed to our table trying to offer a deal. My lawyer surprised me and gave him a talk to the hand. My charges were dropped and Jimmy picked up the murder charge. He was still out on bond until sentencing, though. I walked out the court room to the media and stood behind the podium.

"I'm partnering with the National coalition against domestic violence. One in four women will experience domestic violence in their life time. One point three million women every year are physically assaulted. Children who witness domestic violence will be twice as likely to get abused or be the abuser. One third of female homicides are committed by their partner. One in twelve women have been stalked. It's time for us to break the cycle. I was beat, my mother got beat and her mother was beat. I'm doing everything in my power to stop this societal lie that it's not that serious."

The crowd clapped and whistled as I walked away. Over the next week I worked on programs to open up when you couldn't get help from the police. I knew there were loopholes in Jimmy's case and he might walk. I didn't think about him anymore, he wasn't brave enough to come around when I was an advocate now for domestic violence and stalking. I fired the security that circled my yard daily and erased the fear. I started attending counseling of my own so I could truly help others. I started writing pamphlets for victims giving them avenues to get out the relationship. I felt it was my duty on earth to help other victims.

My daughter left her kids dads and moved in with me permanently so I could help raise my grandchildren. I didn't receive the writer of the year award. It was given to David Weaver for his Bankroll Squad series. I knew that was too good to be true but it kept all my books at the tops of the charts from the nomination

I started working with Tyler Perry as a ghost writer for a couple of his television series. I was even asked to recite my poems at presidential event. I frequently visited the White House and now had an infinite bank account. Everything was falling back in place. I was still hurting from losing Bashee but I was happy to say that if it was only a moment I experienced true love.
I understood my purpose. I needed to help others and try to prevent them from going through abuse. I started mentoring children who lost their parents I would tell them my story of being raised a daddy's girl and I watched as he died on my birthday. I would help them get through the pain embracing it instead of covering it. I understood why I went through so much. I had to suffer to get to this place. I had to experience the humiliation, the insecurities, and the doubt.

I was forced to love myself at the lowest point possible and I did. I made it through, my dark cloud was gone. There was a light inside me that took it away. I was blessed and I was a blessing to others. I even decided to try and start dating again and definitely wanted to take my family on some exotic cruises I was traveling the world. I spent too much time inside and I was free to do whatever.

I had heard Jimmy was getting married. He was happy and they were about to have a son. I had a few people reach out to Jimmy for counseling but he declined so I didn't worry about him anymore.

I actually wished him the best. I wasn't equipped to hurt others. My daughter was planning her wedding and taking a stand against gay rights. She was going to be the first legal marriage in our county and it was getting televised. She spoke with parents and children about understanding their feeling about homosexuals. I was so proud of her. I never thought about her situation and I applauded her for being comfortable with who she was.

I was going to Skype my publishers and talk to them about some ideas later. I wanted to turn a few of my books into movies. My mind raced thinking about my future and what was in store. Everything I wrote was self- help, empowering women and children. I reached out to Ronald, my children's father, and talked him into going to counseling. Ronald shared with me that his mother was killed by his father while he lay asleep in her bed. He woke up with blood splattered on his sleeper being only 5 years old. He remembered it though. The counseling helped him. He enrolled in a mechanic's class full time and stop selling drugs. He came to family functions and would spend time with our grandkids. There was a small cottage I was getting built on my property for my mother to live in. My sister and her husband ran the charities I had started and opened up more as time went by. Crime went down in my hometown dramatically from the resource centers. I would see Tony often but we were just friends. I wasn't dating anyone from my past and honestly he felt more like family now.

Jimmy spent all his money on top attorneys. His case was thrown out due to technicalities. Jimmy was on the news walking out the court room and he mouth I love you baby.

I knew he was talking to me, but I brushed it off. I sent my daughter and her kids to Disney World so they could get a break. She had been trying to figure her life out and she wanted some time alone with her kids. As I pulled back up to my drive I could see the door ajar. I went in my purse to get my gun but I left it in the house. Maybe we were just rushing and it wasn't closed all the way. They do that all the time. I had only been gone a few minutes and the airport was a couple blocks away. I was free and I didn't live in fear anymore. I knew I had a higher power carrying me along the way.

As I was walking up to the door I grabbed my mail. There were several letters and checks and another nomination letter for urban poet of the year. It was still hard to believe that I was talented since it came naturally to me. I never knew that my words were changing people's lives. I walked in the front door with my head down reading the letter and Jimmy was sitting pointing semi-automatic gun at me.

TO BE CONTINUED.........................

FROM THE AUTHOR...........

I've learned since I've been older
Always keep your composure
Stand straight like a soldier
Listen to what y'all elders told ya.
Pray all the time and listen for signs.
If u haven't reached your goal continue to grind...
All women have cookies.
Women. Utilize your minds....
When u get caught up be still do your time.
Sometimes it rains so hard...
I can't see the cars
Eyes wide open.
Only can see so far.
All of a sudden.
Everything goes dim
You let go of the wheel and give it to him.
It's not always what we do with ourselves.
It's when we recognize we have always had help
Although this book is over and you got to the end
My life has just started I'm ready to begin
I've met a lot of new people
I've lost a lot of friends
I've reclaimed my soul
Forgiven myself for my sins
I've poured out my heart
Dug deep from within
So happy to have shared so much of my life with you

THANKFUL

I've been blessed with the sight, to see thru no light
I've been touched with so much that I'll leave with no fuss
In my armor and my shield, I shall have no fear
No emotions, keep composure, difficulties end in closure
All the arrows all the darts, and I've been untouched
Kept my faith always feeling, I've been through enough
Almost breaking, never failing, I've always been tough
Makes me question who's been there, through all my stuff
What's the cause, shake it off, and got to keep it moving
On my toes, wide awake, even when imp snoozing
Questions answered, tasks completed, and imp going to the next
Highly favored, a chosen one, always doing my best
The way of the world, the lack of morals have not changed me a bit
Chaotic scenes, like bad dreams, while I quietly sit
Lessons learned, bridges burned, while the clock continues to tick
One chance to prove, this one life, I refuse to lose
Sudden changes, new lessons, realizing my own confessions
Trials and tribe's come full force, while I'm receiving my blessings
Want to know, slow it down, and listen, never in a rush
I've been blessed with the sight to see thru no light
I've been touched with so much that I'll leave with no fuss
Amen.

Aletta H.

Follow Author Aletta H.
Twitter: @authoraletta
IG: authoraletta
FB: https://www.facebook.com/authoralettah

42413782R00098

Made in the USA
Middletown, DE
10 April 2017